"Charlene Baumbich has a special ability
to put the problems and frustrations of parenting into
perspective . . . to find humor and love in family
situations that seem so grim . . . and to show a new
slant on the age-old dilemma of the empty nest."

LENORE PERSONS
Guideposts Book Club Editor

"She cascades sunshine on parenting woes while
writing away any readers' emotional blahs
on a gloomy day. If your adulthood did not bring
parenthood, try this book for amusing insights
into your lost childhood."

The Christian Reader

Charlene Ann Baumbich

DON'T MISS YOUR KIDS!

(they'll be gone
before you know it)

INTERVARSITY PRESS
DOWNERS GROVE, ILLINOIS 60515

InterVarsity Press® is the book-publishing division of InterVarsity Christian Fellowship®, a student movement active on campus at hundreds of universities, colleges and schools of nursing in the United States of America, and a member movement of the International Fellowship of Evangelical Students. For information about local and regional activities, write Public Relations Dept., InterVarsity Christian Fellowship, 6400 Schroeder Rd., P.O. Box 7895, Madison, WI 53707-7895.

All Scripture quotations, unless otherwise indicated, are taken from the HOLY BIBLE, NEW INTERNATIONAL VERSION®. NIV®. Copyright ©1973, 1978, 1984 by International Bible Society. Used by permission of Zondervan Publishing House. All rights reserved.

Cover illustration: Tim Nyberg

ISBN 0-8308-1641-0

Printed in the United States of America

Library of Congress Cataloging-in-Publication Data

Baumbich, Charlene Ann. 1945-
    Don't miss your kids/Charlene Ann Baumbich.
      p.   cm.
    "Saltshaker books."
    ISBN 0-8308-1331-4 (hdbk.)
    1. Parenting—Religious aspects—Christianity. 2. Baumbich,
Charlene Ann, 1945-   . 3. Parents—United States. I. Title.
BV4529.B38   1991
649'.7—dc20   90-27667
                                          CIP

17	16	15	14	13	12	11	10	9	8	7	6	5	4	3	2	1
07	06	05	04	03	02	01	00	99	98	97	96	95	94			

"Her children arise and call her blessed"
Proverbs 31:28

Dedicated to the
memory of:

My mother
Nellie Ruth Landers Brown
who did not miss her kids.

Acknowledgments

"I thank my God every time I remember you; In all my prayers for all of you, I always pray with joy. . . ."
Philippians 1:3-4

I give paramount thanks to my husband, George, for his divine patience, support and love. Without the unselfish freedom he gave me daily to pursue this labor of love, it wouldn't have happened. God bless him for living with dust balls and eating so many haphazard meals throughout much of this book-writing experience. Truly, many of those hurried casseroles were gross.

To my sons and untiring encouragers, Bret and Brian, I extend heartfelt gratitude. It was when they started calling me "Mom, the writer," that I believed I was one. I'd also like to thank them for supplying me with such good material and bravely allowing me to share it—the good, the bad and the dubious.

Thanks to Rodney Clapp for getting this book started by asking me what was on my mind.

Grateful thanks to Don Stephenson, my "Keep Writin'!" editor, for corralling and channeling what was on my mind—no small task.

His calming approach to my hysterical phone calls, and his sensitivity to my message and struggles were grace upon grace.

Thanks also to:

My father, Victor Wilson Brown, for teaching me to joyfully explore and drink in the world around me;

Mary Gingell for her belief in me, even way back when;

Marlene Fenske for graciously suffering through—by listening to—every trial and triumph along the way;

Mary Beth Elgass for teaching me by Spirit-filled example so much about life;

Al and Barb Unger, Russ and Doris Nelson, and Micky Jackson for celebrating the small victories with me that enabled me to plod on throughout this arduous task;

Jane Scoville for nurturing a budding desire;

Arbor Hill workshop members for their continued and energizing interest in the project;

Elizabeth Cody Newenhuyse and Susan Elizabeth Phillips for their reassurance and mentoring; and

Victor Bianchi at Software City for graciously bailing me out of numerous computer snafus, never once making me feel like the computer stupid I am.

Each behind-the-scenes person at InterVarsity Press who affected this book in one way or another—from the receptionist who fielded my calls, to the artist who symbolized my message, to the person who made sure the last period was in place—has my undying appreciation.

Thanks to countless others who have unknowingly blessed me with a smile or kind word, just when I needed one the most.

To family and friends I give thanks; to God I give the glory.

•

Dear Dixie,

Thanks for the memories.

You turned out to be

the best horse I ever had the

nerve to ride bareback.

Also, you taught me a lot

of good stuff.

•

· One ·

A Disappearing Act

Fleeting Time

It was one of the longest mornings in history, even though I am a morning person. I was scared beyond belief. What if I called James's home and he wasn't there?

I could picture his frozen grammar-school body lying in a shallow ditch, somewhere along the two-block path that led from our house to his. Never in my wildest nightmares did I dream my son, along with his best friend, could be responsible for someone's death. "Children Who Kill!" Didn't Oprah do a program on that once?

The morning had started typically enough. I was in the kitchen by myself—always the first to rustle and rise on a Saturday—putting tea water on. It was going to be another gloomy Chicago winter day. Temperatures had dropped to about fifteen below zero during the night. I surveyed our back yard through the kitchen window and pondered how frigid everything looked. The stark, white birch branches appeared brittle, as did the frozen steel pole to the bird feeder.

But things were toasty inside. Visions of Super Mom danced in my head as I decided to make home-made pancakes for my younger son, Brian, and his two sleep-over pals, Bob and James.

I was feeling not only clever but rather perky since I'd had a good night's sleep. Unusual for a sleep-over. It doesn't take much to awaken me; the boys must have conked out early, I suspected.

George shuffled his way into the kitchen. "Boys still sleeping?" he asked.

"I heard some mumbling up there," I answered. "They'll probably be down soon. I'm gonna make pancakes for breakfast." (Tadah!) He instructed me to call him when breakfast was ready, then down the stairs he headed for his weekend rearrange-the-basement project.

It wasn't long before Bob appeared. Probably the rattling of the pans lured him out of his sleeping bag.

"Good morning, Mrs. Baumbich."

"Good morning, Bob." He eyed the box of Bisquick (okay, *almost* home-made pancakes) and the griddle, then pulled out a chair and sat down at the table.

"Sleep well?" I queried. He didn't look like it.

"Okay, I guess." End of discussion. But then how much do sixth-grade boys ever have to say to someone else's mom?

Then Brian came out of his bedroom and headed straight for the floor in front of the living room television. Cartoons. Bob whisked in behind him and draped himself across the couch. I peeked up the stairs to Brian's bedroom door. Thought I'd welcome James to

Saturday morning at the Baumbichs' house, but the door was closed. He must still be sleeping.

About twenty minutes passed and the pancakes hit the table.

"Come and get it, everyone," I hollered into the basement and around the corner, trying to override the cartoon noise. "Somebody go wake up James."

Within a minute everyone was seated at the table. Everyone except James. "Somebody go get James," I repeated.

"He's not here," Brian casually responded.

"He's not here? Where is he?" my husband asked.

"Home," Brian said.

"What in the world time did he call his mother? Before dawn?" I asked.

"He didn't call his mother. He walked home last night. Pass the pancakes," Brian said without missing a beat or batting an eye.

"Walked home! Last night?" I squeaked out. My heart was pounding. "What time? Why?"

"Because I told him to go home," Brian said flatly.

"Good grief, Brian! It's fifteen below zero!"

"So, he had a coat."

"What time did he leave?" George asked. His voice sounded somewhere near the pitch of mine.

"About twelve or one or something. Maybe it was eleven. I don't remember."

"Why did you tell him to leave?" I asked.

"Because he got boogers on my sleeping bag."

By this time I thought I was going to hyperventilate. It was time to stop this discussion and find out if James had made it home. I didn't know whether to get in the car and start cruising the ditches or pick up the phone and call Linda, James's mother.

"Call Linda," George said.

"Brian!" I screeched on my way to the phone. "How could you do such a thing? Did James even have a hat? He could be frozen to death somewhere. Were his parents even home?"

Bob sat silent all this while, eyes glued to the empty plate before him.

As I dialed the number, my mind churned along with my stomach. How could I have let this happen? What will Linda think when I call her and ask her if James is home when he's supposed to be at my house? What if he isn't there?

Ring. Ring. Ring. Ring. Ring.

"Hello," a groggy voice finally said.

"Hello. This is Charlene. I can't believe I'm asking you this question," I said, trying to find the courage to get out the words. "Is James home?"

"Yes. He came home in the middle of the night. Didn't you know that?"

I deserve to die, I thought. What in the world kind of mother am I. "No," I finally answered. "Oh, Linda. I'm so sorry. I had no idea. Was James okay?"

"Cold. But okay. He said Brian kicked him out."

Just shoot me right here and now, I thought. Where did I go wrong in my parenting that a son of mine could kick a child out into sub-zero temperatures in the middle of the night.

"I'm just getting the story, Linda. I'm so sorry. I'm so relieved James is okay. I cannot apologize enough," I rattled on and on.

"Everything is all okay. Don't worry," she kept assuring. But it wasn't.

"I can't believe Brian would do such a thing! I'm so sorry."

"Charlene. Everything is okay. We'll talk about it later. Right now I want to go back to bed."

"Okay. I'll call you this afternoon. Again, I'm sorry."

Brian sat pounding down pancakes like there was no tomorrow. Bob said he wanted to go home.

"I'll take you, Bob," I said. "Brian, you sit right at this table, young man, until I get back. We're going to talk!"

"About what? James is fine, right?"

"James IS fine, right?" George echoed, needing to validate James's safety.

"Yes," I pelted into the kitchen air that seemed to be choking me, "but that's hardly the point here!"

"I know," George replied. "I'll take Bob home. Brian, listen to your mother."

Great.

Brian finished his pancakes in total silence. I was afraid if I started in, I might kill him—right after I pummeled myself to death with the pancake flipper. I waited for George to return. We pow-wowed.

It was decided we should get all three boys and their parents around the table. There was more than a child's error, here. There was an opportunity to discuss friendships, safety, attitudes, common sense, yielding to authority, responsibility and the reality of a disaster that could have happened. Brian should not have kicked James out. James should not have gone in the middle of the night without informing the people responsible for him, or his parents. Bob should have done whatever he could. They had all made bad choices. And I, for one, really didn't care to discuss the boogers that started it all.

*   *   *

17

This is an example of good, bad and dubious memories rolled into one. It happened a long time ago; that sixth-grader is now a sophomore in college.

Could I lead a happy life without this memory? Yes. Did a bad situation lend an opportunity for growth, not only for the boys, but for our parenting wisdom? Yes. Is "The Night the Boogers Almost Killed James" good fodder for a horror movie? Dubious. Was knowing how to ride bareback a helpful skill in passing through this fire? You bet.

I'll explain that last statement in a minute. Right now, I want to grab you by the shoulders and shake you into awareness. Pay attention. The clock is ticking.

Before you know it, your children have grown and flown. It happens in a finger snap—even though a colicky baby's wailing can make one late afternoon seem a week long. And a stubborn three-year-old simply will not potty train, striking the fear in you that some day his bride may have to change his diapers. And you are convinced you're locked in a time warp with your mouthy adolescent (who just nearly killed someone). And your teenager is two hours late for curfew but it seems like a year because it's after midnight and raining and you're wired from numerous cups of caffeine and . . . hey! I know what it's like; I've been there.

But now I am somewhere else in my life. Oh, my address hasn't changed, but my children are gone. I'm a new empty nester—and loaded with hindsight. You know, that kind of hindsight wherein lies truth. The kind you never have a chance to utilize because the time for its payoff is gone.

A lot of things are gone for me now: first smiles, giggles, drooling kisses, rosy cheeks, first steps, rock collections, paper Valentines, Cub Scout pins, ballet recitals, filled laps. Gone.

Gone too are detentions, sibling quarrels, first cars, summer jobs, slamming doors (except, perhaps, for an occasional one of mine), young love, lost glasses, sleep-overs, prom-night jitters, graduation tears. . . . My children—our children—are gone in a finger snap.

There is no dress rehearsal to prepare you for an empty nest. There is only the journey, which cannot be replayed or redone. By the time your children leave, you have either basked in the essence of their lives or missed it.

What they leave behind is precious memories. All of them: the good, the bad and the dubious. All of them we are there to collect, that is.

This isn't a book meant to give you one more thing to do, one more burden to carry. Although my message is urgent, my hope is that the impact of it will lighten your load, for now and for the rest of your days. Child rearing is always with us, whether we're simply anticipating and planning for the little darlings, trying to keep our heads out of the quicksand of the terrible twos, or living with the remnants. So the way I see it, we might as well simply learn to ride bareback.

*   *   *

Being raised on a small farm, I had occasion to barrel race on a cutting horse named Dixie. I see direct similarities between raising a child and riding a beast bareback. Forget about blankets and saddles and fancy tack, just hop on and gently neck-rein the critter. Appreciate the high-spiritedness that excites you yet gives you caution. Hug real hard to keep from sliding under its belly and getting trampled. Learn to anticipate the corners and lean into them for balance. Sometimes let the horse have the reins. Know when it's time to head for the barn. Be willing to turn the horse out to pasture

19

when it's too old for you to ride.

Yes, both bareback riding and parenting are earthy and bold adventures.

In these pages I'd like to share with you some of my memories— about our children, not Dixie. They range from "Triumph!" to "Egads!" I present them not just to hear myself rattle (although my children *and* husband tell me I occasionally have that tendency), but in hopes that through them you will see the importance of embracing these years with your children. Think about it: if I hadn't been paying attention, these pages would be empty. As empty as my heart would be.

But fortunately for me, my child-rearing days were filled with gathering every emotional keepsake I was capable of. Oh, I'm sure my two boys, Bret and Brian, participated in lots of things that my husband and I will never know about . . . thank goodness.

And don't get me wrong, all our memories are not rosy. We have served our time in the trenches, thereby earning all the super-glued trinkets, humiliating experiences and looming regrets we are entitled to. But whether exhausting or uplifting, if memorable moments were there for the taking, we grabbed them and tucked them away like the treasures they are. For that, I will be eternally grateful.

As I openly wept and waved good-bye to my baby, a five-foot, ten-inch, handsome male with a good sense of himself—despite some parental blunders along the way—I knew life would never be the same. Leaving him there without a single friend, two whole states away and in the care of an unfamiliar college, the five-hour ride home seemed like an endless bridge. A transition journey to unfamiliar territory: a home with no children. It was a scary ride.

But along with the sense of loss there welled an overwhelming thankfulness that I had not missed my children. I wanted to leap out of the car, hurl myself up on the hood with a bull horn and roar to the heavens: "Thank you! Thank you, God, that through some blessed instinct, I knew there would be plenty of time one day for me, and here it is.

"Thank you that I was raised by parents who knew how to *play* and passed on that blessing! Thank you for choices I made along the way, as difficult as many of them were. Choices that put me on the little league parade route with my camera; in front of the principal with humility; in the bleachers with gut-wrenching tension; at the YMCA with eau-de-chlorine; in the emergency room with pure fright; on a blanket in the park with a picnic basket; in a car packed to the gills with worms, hooks, bobbers and fishing poles. All those places where I will remember being *with* my children. Enduring. Celebrating. Holding my breath. Relishing. Wishing time would freeze."

But time does not freeze. Only in the truth of hindsight do you really get a grip on how quickly it passes. Each event you are experiencing—or missing—will never happen again.

When tears and prayers of thankfulness were winding down on that ride home from college, I found a pulsating, urgent message started filling the quiet.

Wake up, parents! I wanted to scream. In a finger snap your kids will be gone! You cannot get these years back! Give yourself permission to enjoy them while you can. Study and recapture for yourself your child's eagerness. Stroke and inhale the fragrance of their perfect creation. Appreciate the adult blossoming in each of them. Let your house ring with laughter. Believe that troubled times will pass, because they do; take stock and learn to value even those bumpy roads, because they, too, may be remembered as precious milestones. Know that now you are setting the groundwork for your relationship with your children when they are grown.

So many of today's parents are filled with pressure to wear so many hats, raise "gifted" and perfect children and "have it all," that they are, I am afraid, missing what is before them. Priceless, fleeting years lost in the busy shuffle. How, I wonder, will they endure the blank pages in their personal scrapbooks. They will finger snap to an empty nest, pull out their portfolio of memories and weep for its emptiness. Don't let this be you.

I once heard someone say, "Nobody on a deathbed ever wished they had spent more time at the office."

On a similar note, Dan Zedan carries in his wallet a business-size card that has become tattered from all its years of viewing. An eighty-six-year-old scoutmaster gave it to him a long time ago hoping it would perk him up; Zedan had just become a Boy Scout leader.

"In a hundred years it will not matter what my bank account was, the sort of house I lived in or the kind of car I drove," the card reads. "But the world may well be different because I was important in the life of a boy."

Although Zedan, father of five, doesn't know who wrote those words, they've penetrated his life as well as the lives of countless others he has shared them with.

Both thoughts reflect the same message: Priorities. Will they, in the long haul, lead you to fulfillment, or fill you with regrets? Now, while the children are with you, is the time to consider the options. Later, they have passed you by.

"Behold," the psalmist said, "children are a gift of the Lord," and all too soon they are gone.

•

Attention Kmart shoppers:
We have a lost mother
in the store. If you should
find her, be kind,
then point her toward home.

•

· *Two* ·

In the Beginning

Disillusionment

Visions *of wonderment begin to dance in our heads when word* comes that we are "with child." Nowadays you can find out nearly minutes after conception with over-the-counter, do-it-yourself tests. Back in my child-bearing years, however, endless months, millions of anxious, strung-together moments had to crawl by before we "officially" knew that visions of wonderment could, indeed, begin to run rampant.

Baby at Mom's breast. Dad's arm around the two of them, parental heads leaning together. Tiny fingers wrapped around larger, caring ones. The sound of a music box tinkling in the background. "Essence of Baby" fragrance that always smells like baby powder. Husband and wife perched over the softened crib pondering with adoring eyes their little sleeping bundle of perfection.

The future beckons. Finger paintings mounted with the respect of a Picasso adorn the refrigerator door. Notes from school explain that Johnny is not only the smartest child in the class but also the most polite. Best batting average on the baseball team. C.E.O. Captain of a major airline who gives free passes to Mom and Dad for world travel. A six-foot-ten quarterback for the Chicago Bears who leads his team to Superbowl Victory, then grins and waves into the camera while mouthing "Hi, Mom and Dad. Thanks for the perfect life we've had!"

And then we give birth.

*　　*　　*

All those Lamaze classes. I couldn't stop thinking about all that "natural" stuff I was prepared to endure. Prepared? Right! I lie groggy in the recovery room. Recovering not only from birthing my second son who weighed in a healthy eight-pound, two-ounce little porker, but from a hypodermic shot, a local, an anesthesiologist holding a gas mask over my face. . . .

Oh sure, I witnessed the birth of my son, but not without pre- and post-problems. Not without screaming at my husband who was also prepared (?) for my possible (?) uncontrollable nastiness. Not without somehow feeling like I'd blown it. I'd been through this unprepared once before—weren't things supposed to be different this time?

But hey, that was behind me now. I could concentrate on re-kindling my wonderment. I could just lie here and be waited on and ooh and aah our new bundle. I could fantasize about how this little cherub would behave even better than the first, were that humanly possible. (Not only did I forget the pains of childbirth from my first son, but other things I didn't want to remember as well.) I could envision the bonding and blessings passed between parents and child and between little brothers. I could rest assured that I was older this time, wiser, more mature, more patient and in complete control.

And then we took him home.

It wasn't long before reality gripped me by the throat and, much to my horror, I wanted to grab our precious, screaming little bundle the same way! And how about that five-year-old brother of his? Wasn't it about time he settled down?

Not that we didn't have splendid moments in the beginning; we had many. We were even occasionally visited by good days. But much of that first three to four months had to be endured, plowed through and led by a frenzied brain that simply did not get enough sleep. Scenes like the following snap into view as I recollect this passage of our lives.

It is late afternoon and supper is supposed to be cooking. I am supposed to be cooking it. Instead, I am holding a baby who has been screaming for twenty minutes straight. I am rocking him back and forth, gently bouncing him up and down, and patting his back for a burp I'm sure is lodged in there sideways and simply can't escape. I am staring out the window, down the road, in the direction from which my husband's car should be appearing any moment. PLEASE!

Bret is in his bedroom where I have sent him for the eleventy hundredth time this particular day. He is grounded—and, it occurs to me, so am I.

I remind myself that this was our choice. Our vision. Our plan. Our wonderment (egads!). I remind myself I hated baby-sitting when I was a young girl. This should have been a clue. Perhaps I should have converted and joined a convent.

Too late. This is reality. Reality: elation seasoned with heavy doses of exhaustion, despair and disillusionment. Wonderment be darned!

And then I hear it. My husband's key to our home-sweet-home is slipping into the keyhole. I also hear Bret's bedroom door squeak open and I see one half of his eye, nose and mouth risking a peek.

"Get back in there!" I demand. I fly down the stairs like Scarlett O'Hara toward Rhett, except instead of a billowing skirt accompanying me, it's a bellowing kid. I reach the entryway just in time to see my husband open the door.

"Here!" I bark. "Take your son! I have got to get out of here before I explode or kill somebody!"

"Bad day, huh?" he counters, as he sets his briefcase down and takes in a deep breath.

"Bret's in his room where he should stay until he draws a pension!"

"What's wrong with my little Brian?" my husband asks as he gently peels the hysterical mass from the crazed me and cuddles him into his own calm arms.

"Your guess is as good as mine!" I can not talk normally. I can only scream. "He's nursed five times in the last two hours. I feel like nothing but a dairy cow! His pants are dry, unless, of course, he peed them in the last thirty seconds, which he probably did because that's all he's done all day!"

"Where are you going," my husband calmly asks while his massive hand gently strokes Brian's back.

"I don't know. China. The snack bar in Kmart."

"When will you be back?"

"I don't know. Maybe never."

"What's for supper?"

"Whatever you can find."

The door closes behind me.

The door re-opens in thirty seconds. It is cold. I have no coat. No purse. No car keys. I scurry around collecting them, slamming closet and cabinet doors behind me.

I notice on my way back out that the house is full of the sounds of . . . quiet. George is sitting on the couch with Brian resting on his lap. He is talking softly to him, directly to him, their faces are not a foot apart. Brian coos. Bret's door squeaks. It is obvious he was on his way down to greet a much-welcomed Dad until Mom lodged her sneak re-entry.

For a brief moment, I consider staying. But I don't.

*   *   *

Although this is hardly one of my proudest memories, yet I find it is filled with grace. Amazing, undeserved grace. I recognize it as such because one of the most valuable arts a parent can possess, in my opinion, surfaced at that heated moment like the surprise of a refreshing wind gust—and no, it was not flying the coop!

It is the art of capturing the pristine moments. Those experiences that unleash flashes of truth. Those moments that envelop us with God's presence in our children and ourselves. Crystallized flashes that imprint divine blessings on our hearts. Imprints we can call forth from memory, afterward, to carry us through the rough times.

Pure grace. We need only be still enough to receive it.

*   *   *

The Fox River silently slips by in the background. We relax at a prime-location picnic table under a grove of trees in Pottawatomie Park, St. Charles, Illinois. We *finally* relax, that is. Earlier on this Saturday we had to spring out of bed in order to start preparing and loading up for this pleasure: Weber grill, charcoal, charcoal lighter, cooking utensils, at least two coolers, disposable diapers, Frisbee, ball and bat, fishing tackle, radio, playpen, playing cards, lawn chairs, suntan lotion, mosquito repellent, board games, toilet paper (just in case), a watermelon. . . . We met our friends there at 10:30 a.m. in order to stake our claim to this fine location—our friends who brought along just as much stuff as we did, perhaps even more since they were a child up on us.

It was one of those days when you couldn't help but feel the rays of the sun penetrate and light up your very core. A slight breeze rustled the leaves and curled around our eyebrows. It was neither hot nor cold; it was perfection. And it was a miracle: the children got along all day, except for a few minor mishaps that weren't important enough to raise a voice over.

Dusk snuck up on the river; our belongings were packed and ready to go. Two meals behind us, satisfaction swelled and took a foothold.

Brian was conked out in his playpen. He slept soundly, cheek resting on the corner of his blue "blankie" with the satin edge, thumb anchored securely in his mouth, toddler lungs full up with fresh air, knees drawn up under him. I ever-so-gently stroked the side of his cheek with the back of my index finger. His grip caressed his favorite portion of the satin and he faintly suckled and grinned.

The darkened outline of Bret's skinny little form sat squat along the bank, fishing pole extended in front of him. He was far from a patient child; this moment of stillness was rare and inspiring. In his squat little shadow, in this moment of dusk, I was suddenly washed through with warmth: how fragile are his feelings. How freely he loves; how quickly he forgives. How blessed am I to be his mother.

George sat off to the side with Al. They were talking quietly about something. Chuckles burst and disappeared like the light of the fireflies they mingled with.

There was time to stay a while longer. And we did.

*   *   *

This was a pristine moment that fluttered upon me like the butterfly of happiness. I would have had a hard time fighting it off. But sometimes the art of capturing—let alone even seeing—those pristine moments is elusive at best. We need to aggressively seek them, condition ourselves to spot them, and cling to their sanity-saving capabilities when we find them.

In case you missed it, just before Miss Drama here made her exit to Kmart, she seized one of those moments, even though she couldn't—and I mean COULD NOT—stay to applaud it. But she, I, seized it and tucked it away. It would be what enabled me to return.

But there were other things I needed to do first. I needed to depart. I knew my children were safe and in good hands. I shot an arrow prayer up to God thanking him for such a faithful and understanding husband who allowed me to back off from the situation so I could gain some perspective. Time to calm down. Time to think. Time to remember. I needed to reverse out of my driveway so rapidly that the tires spit gravel in all directions.

Next I needed to get a grip on safe driving while crying and screaming at the same time. Then the toughest task: finding a place to go. Girlfriends' houses were out; they all have kids. Kmart would simply have to do. After intensely aiming the cart down every aisle in the store and occasionally even hurling something in, I started winding down. Eventually, I made my way to the food area. Lingering over a diet drink and french fries, I was coming to the end of what I needed to do. Had to do to keep from exploding. Perfectly normal and relatively harmless behavior for me.

And something I advise for others. Not my particular routine, perhaps; it might not work for you. But you must find your own harmless routine that calms you down. Learn to accept overwrought, emotional moments as normal periods in any parent's life. We do, after all, have feet of clay, not Novocain.

What happened while I was downing the fries and cola, however, is what allowed me to return. I pulled out that image of my husband and Brian: face to face, serene, giving love to one another. It was a reminder that all child-rearing is not screaming kids and bad behavior, including mine. In fact, if we were to graph it I'm sure those times would be in the minority.

Then I envisioned half of my older son's little face peeking at me. Hoping the dust had settled. Wanting a hug. Needing to know that I still loved him even though it had been a rough day for all of us.

I recalled first rides on merry-go-rounds, bouquets of dandelions, ripples of three-month-old smiles, the feel of the silky hair on the top of a baby's head nestling under my chin, the sweat dripping down my husband's face at the altar . . . I remembered that I loved them all, and that included their bad and dubious behavior as well as the pristine. I needed them. They needed me.

I returned to the images I held on to (lasting truth), not the disaster I had left behind (temporary). It was an anxious ride home and a humble entrance. Brian still squawked a little at bedtime and Bret had not been transformed into wonder boy, but that was okay. I was okay. We would, indeed, all be okay.

*   *   *

Daniel Taylor recently revealed in an article for *Marriage Partnership* magazine that for him and wife Jayne their fourth child, Anne, came as a surprise. Their youngest child at that time was already nine years old.

"To be honest," he wrote, "I think I have sometimes felt a mild and unfocused resentment about the whole thing. 'Resentment' is too strong, but it suggests the sense of being put upon.

" 'I shouldn't have to be doing this,' part of me says. 'I've given lots of time and energy to getting three kids off to a good start; why should I have to do it a fourth time? Why does this come along just when I thought I was going to have more time and energy to write?'

"But then I look," he continued, "really look, at our baby, Anne.

"And what do I see? I see another bit of eternity dropped into our lives. I see something that will last forever, a God-given human spirit, making its first contact with the world. And in watching her, I am drawn away from the illusory world of getting and spending and accomplishing, and back to the real world of mind and spirit and love."

So, it is in looking, really looking, and in remembering, and calling to memory, that we find the often hidden blessings of parenting. Blessings that hide behind stress. Gifts that can easily become camouflaged by disillusionment, even though disillusionment seems to be a normal part of the parental cycle. In reality, that child, that gift from God, is no less a gift when he or she is screaming in a soggy diaper than when the newly bathed infant is all cuddly and smell-good; it is rather just not the way our wonderment pictured it.

And so, as difficult as it is, we would do well to listen to the words in the epistle of James when he advises us to "consider it ALL joy." Not just the obvious pleasures, But ALL of it. "In

EVERYTHING give thanks," Paul said in Thessalonians. Everything—including disillusionment.

* * *

Sometimes I find that the "calling to memory" portion of my philosophy needs a little help. Memories have a way of blurring at the edges, softening a bit. Like the perfect behavior I wanted to remember in Bret, when I was in the hospital having Brian. The "wonderment" memory.

Other times, however, recollections have a way of flat out getting confused. Take the two monstrous boxes of photographs we have crammed in a certain closet. Very few have dates on them. Most developed roles of film have, over the years, gotten shuffled with other roles as we scrambled through them searching for "the time. . . ." And we are aghast to find we have forgotten many of the details surrounding these visual slices of life. Oh sure, we can tell one child from another, but how old, exactly, was that child? What grade was he in? Whose birthday party was this? Where in the world were we? Who are those people in the background? I'm sure I never had that dorky hairdo!

The fact of the matter is, like putting saddle soap and leather conditioner on the reins to keep them from dry rotting, so it is necessary to date and validate photographs to overcome the dry rot of memory. Trust me, where memory fails, bold print takes over. It's the same with those wonderful baby books we accept at showers with the best of intentions. "We'll write it down later," whatever "it" may be, far too often translates into writing it down wrong or never. It's unfortunate George and I didn't learn this little gem until we owned a closet full of "guesstiments."

You may think this is crazy. You may say to yourself, "How

could I ever forget this?" as you laugh your way through your latest batch of snapshots or videos. But batches of things have a way of multiplying, like slugs under a flower pot. Even though you don't think this will happen to you, you may be grateful twenty years from now when you can prove beyond a shadow of a doubt that yes indeed, one of your family members did wear his pants hiked up that high when he was four years old!

Then again, some slices of life need no photographs, no labeling or even nudges to remain forever perfectly focused in your mind. To draw them forth elicits the same emotion that surrounded them the first time.

*   *   *

Eighteen years after I left my screaming baby in the arms of my husband to seek the shelter of Kmart, that same eight-pound, two-ounce baby boy's high-school graduation day arrived. I cannot believe it. My baby graduating.

I sit in my office with the door closed, weeping and writing him a letter while he dresses for the ceremony. So much I must say to him. So much I need to say to him. So little time to capture my thoughts before we leave for the school.

"Even though I've had since the day you were born to prepare for this," I type, "I find I'm running behind."

I sit and stare at the blinking cursor. How can I sum up eighteen years of love? Eighteen years of good, bad and dubious memories? How can I express in words how proud I am?

I hear him summon his father to make sure the knot in his tie is just right, a task he can actually handle quite well alone. Flashes of photographs rip through my mind: a little boy wearing a crooked clip-on tie making it appear as if the wind is blowing when in fact it is not; a nervous young man readying for his first high-school dance who wants to make sure he looks as perfect as possible. Each photograph reveals the steady and reassuring hands of a father; his child's face, very close to his own—not unlike the face-to-face vision I carried out my door that harried day. Faces that mirror the resemblances: eyebrows, chin line, nose and that beckoning smile.

Through blurred vision, walls and time I see this familiar scenario taking place in my son's room. Perhaps this is the last time it will ever be repeated. I see the mobile gently circling over his crib and study the look of awe and wonder on his baby face. I feel his tiny hand gently pummeling my breast as he nurses. I hear the faint utterances of "da-da" and "ma-ma." I celebrate that first stumbling step he took out of my arms. I pray that God will forever hold close my baby who is readying to face the world without us at his side.

Words finally fill the page—some coaxed out of a tight throat, others pouring forth unbridled. I sign the letter with my fountain pen reserved for the most important of occasions. I carefully fold these pieces of my heart and tuck them under the ribbon I have tied around a kite. A gift I bought to present to him as a rose is presented to an opera singer as a gift of appreciation and heartfelt gratitude. The watch will come later; the kite is symbolic of the little boy I don't want to become lost in a man. The little boy I hope never forgets how to play—and I've told him this in my letter.

We arrive very early at the outdoor graduation site so we can secure premium seats in the bleachers—not unlike efforts to claim that favored picnic location. It is a beautiful day. The bleachers at Glenbard West High School overlook not only the football field where the ceremony will take place, but the lovely backdrop of Lake Ellyn surrounded by picturesque trees.

My husband keeps postponing handing me the program. I find

it curious behavior but I am too busy purposefully capturing every detail of this scene to let it bother me. Finally the ceremony begins.

There are a few words of welcome and then it is announced that four voices from the choir of the Glenbard West High School class of 1989 will sing, a cappella, the national anthem. Brian steps onto the platform with three other young adults. This is the first I know of his surprise—this perfect of gifts—for his mother.

Their voices ring clearly in the stillness. My son's eyes scan the crowd and lock on mine. His lips move to the words; his bass voice is strong and pure. His eye winks. At me. Directly at me.

I am filled with wonderment. Wonderment beyond my imagination. True wonderment that is forever captured and locked in my memory. A vision I will usher forth many times during the lonely days after he has left for college.

Dear Diary,
Today I learned how to tie
the magic bow that
keeps a shoelace from coming
untied. Yippee! My baby's
a sophomore in high school.

· *Three* ·

All We Don't Know about Parenting

Incompetence

June 1979. Last day of school. This mother's delight—and torment. Delight that the nightly homework hassle is behind us for a few months, and parts of our harried schedule can take a nap. Torment because my last day of personal freedom until fall is drawing to a close.

There's a decision to be made here: should I be busily cleaning on this last of child-free days for a while? Nah. I should be sitting in the back yard amongst the flowers, sipping tea, reading or just staring into space. And that's precisely what I do.

I ponder the fact that Bret is experiencing his final day as an eighth grader. Major transitions lie ahead, for him and for me. For Bret, manhood looms around the corner. But first he must pass through another transition fire: going from being the eighth-grade hot shot to once again ranking lowest on the totem pole in a different school. As for George and me, we must help keep his self-esteem intact during this stormy period as well as allow him some room to be an adolescent—a difficult stage for everyone involved.

It also occurs to me I can no longer simply say what grades my boys are in when queried; I must refer to them as "a third grader and a freshman in high school."

Freshman! What year is this? I prop my tea glass in the grass next to my lawn chair and head for the bathroom mirror. After a couple minutes of jowl and crows' feet inspection I decide things aren't too bad yet. Besides, why waste these precious moments worrying anyway? I resume my laid-back post.

While I am watching cloud formations, Bret is manning home plate during a softball game at school. Steve Wasnick is pitching. There is a play at the plate. Wasnick whips the ball to Bret who immediately drops it because pain shoots through his thumb the second the ball smacks into it.

The runner is safe. Bret is sent to the nurse. She deems it possibly broken. School is almost out for the day, however, so she ices it for a while, advises him to be careful of his throbbing digit and ride the bus home as usual. Of course he is to tell his mother that she, the nurse, believes his thumb should be x-rayed. Upon his arrival home he does so, abruptly ending my freedom.

Before I deal with the thumb, however, I quickly thank God for the wisdom he granted me to know when it was time to stockpile a refreshing little rest instead of scurrying around spit-shining. I just love it when daydreaming wins! Especially when it beats out ring-around-the-collar calisthenics. "Thank you, God," I say, "for this profound discovery!" Now, back to the hand in my face.

I carefully inspect his thumb, the way I have inspected dozens of other injured limbs of both my children over the years. It looks slightly swollen, but then so do his eyes. So does a sprain. So does a mosquito bite or a good wallop.

He sighs as he reads my mind, the mind he has eventually heard spoken every other time this scenario has played.

"How badly does it hurt?" I always ask them. "It's probably not broken. We'll just go sit in the clinic for hours while they shuffle us from urgent care to x-ray and back again," I whine. "Then the doctor will finally tell us nothing is wrong and we will receive a very large bill and by tomorrow you will forget it even hurt." Not once has anything actually been broken.

But we always go anyway because I don't know what a broken anything really looks like, and my conscience starts riding me, and I love my children and I don't want them to heal with crooked limbs.

For the record, it has also been proven that I do not consistently know the difference between postnasal drip and bronchitis. How many times, I wonder, has Brian snorted and snotted around, running a slight temperature on and off, keeping us (mostly me) up at night, only for us (always me) to become convinced he will surely die without some of that pink medicine. And so I sit next to my phone in the early hours with bleary eyes haunting the clock, waiting for the appointment lines to open.

Off we finally go. Sometimes we get pink medicine or a shot. During these times I commend my intuitive self. Except, of course, for the time I sent him to school after a check-up and a throat culture because he had no temperature and seemed perfectly fine but for a scratchy throat. And don't you know the lab called and said it was strep!

But other times we are informed of a mere cold, postnasal drip, or less. And we pay our bill. And I file the episode in my memory bank for the next bout. Just like I file the "nothing-is-broken" messages we've always received. Try chicken soup and Popsicles first, I tell myself. Wait a couple days and see what transpires, I coax.

But now, this last-of-eighth-grade day, Bret stands before me, thumb presented like a royal jewel to a queen. I express my sympathy and look appropriately sad. He still thinks it's broken. I soften my usual lecture. He sighs again and endures, but doesn't become dissuaded. I wear down and take him to the clinic.

After the predicted waits between shufflings, we finally watch the doctor ceremoniously mount two very large black-and-white bits of evidence on a lighted screen. He carefully studies them, moving his head between the two. Next, he pulls a ball-point pen out of his pocket.

"Right here," he says, using the pen for a pointer, "is a slight fracture. We'll get a splint on that and it should heal just fine."

Bret jumps up in the air and screams, "Did you hear that, Mom? It's broken! It's really broken!" He grins from ear to ear as he dances around me celebrating, right there in the doctor's office. A doctor, who, I might add, seems a bit puzzled at the reaction.

I can't say I was happy, but somehow I was momentarily justified as a mother. A mother who made the right move this particular day.

And there was another happy person: Steve Wasnick. The next day Bret ran into him at a carnival. When Bret confirmed the implications of the metal and green-foam splint he was wearing like a medal of honor, the two of them did a high five. Wasnick was overjoyed that he could throw a ball fast enough to break someone's thumb!

Even Brian was happy. Although he got no immediate pleasure out of the ordeal, he knew that from this day forward he would have something to remind Mom about the next time she started her "I'm-sure-it's-nothing" lecture.

*   *   *

I am convinced that all parents struggle through bouts of feeling incompetent. Why don't I know this stuff? I've asked myself on many occasions. Why are so many things that happen to us not covered in the manuals?

Why if it worked for one kid isn't it working for the other? Are my instinct mechanisms broken? Does this little episode carry enough of its own consequences, or do I need to bring in some reinforcements? Will they settle the disagreement by themselves or will they draw blood? Is he telling me the truth? What happens when we parents disagree on an approach?

Now there's no point beating ourselves up for asking these questions; we *should* ask them. By the same token, we need to be careful we don't get swept away by confusion and doubt. We can become so focused on the trial and anxiety of it all that we miss our kids.

Our sense of incompetence can bring on panic attacks which in turn produce certain hallucinations:

HEADLINE: "Five-year-old boy stays awake for three consecutive days while father has nose stuck in books reading about the advantages and disadvantages of making your children take naps."

HEADLINE: "Toddler crawls unsupervised to top of Sears Tower while mother stands in trance-like state in front of ground-floor elevator debating the advisability of exposing her child to such a swift ascent in a confined area. She was last heard mumbling something about the possible death of her intuition."

HEADLINE: "Children run around neighborhood naked and starving while parents argue about whether or not children should wear only non-synthetic fabrics and maintain tofu diets."

Why is it we think everyone will hear about our mistakes?

There are times, however, when I marvel at my spontaneous aptitude. Just the right response. The most appropriate of disciplines. A great sense of fine tuning that enables me to read behind the words. A hug that heals. At these moments, I am fervently grateful to God for building in the skills and giving me the life experiences that enable me to be a good mother.

But basically I have to rely on God's promises and grace to carry my children through, beyond, and in spite of my blind leadings.

It would be hard to imagine raising children without counting on God to guide and instruct me. Without his presence and Spirit granting me patience, endurance and acceptance of circumstances beyond my control, I would surely be bonkers by now.

I remind myself often that he, God, is Love. He loves my children more than I am even capable of understanding the word. He loves me just as much, for I am also his child. Aren't we all in wonderful hands? And so during times of utter panic when it comes to parental decisions, I claim his promises: "I can do everything through him who gives me strength" (Phil 4:13); "In this world you will have trouble. But take heart! I have overcome the world" (Jn 16:33b).

I truly believe that if God has overcome the world, he can help me overcome the evils of potty training. I can count on him to help me know when it's time to back off. He will deliver me from prideful mistakes and forgive me for foolish ones, and vice versa. He knows my heart and I pray he will help me have sense enough to give him my will . . . and my children.

We have at our fingertips the most precious of commodities.

That makes parenting a mighty responsibility!

Just watch any of the talk shows to see how many people are blaming their messed-up lives on their parents. Just check the book stores for the swelling wave of how-to volumes about parenting, so much of it guilt-producing. I say guilt-producing because there's no way any of us can do everything they tell us to. In fact, much of what we read is in conflict within the genre. There are so many armies of warnings and directions being delivered to our browsing faces that we could easily become convinced nothing about parenting is natural—or fun. We could become neurotic and gridlocked with fear. We could forget that God calls us to be joyful.

Should we become caught in the snare of expectations of perfect parenting, we would, without a doubt, be missing our kids: we would be so focused on *us* and our abilities that we would miss out on *them* and their gifts. We would not allow room for them to teach us, and their lessons are bountiful, indeed.

We would expect the same perfection from them that we require of ourselves. We would judge our parenting skills solely by our children's behavior, which we all know is sometimes totally out of line, as is our own. We would forget why Christ died: precisely because we are incapable of reaching perfection.

Yes, parenting is crazy-making. But it also is an unequalled opportunity, in my opinion, for us to celebrate the gift of life and the freedom God gives us to ride by the seat of the pants. To cling to him for dear life and trust that he knows where he's taking us and our children.

Not that seeking advice from the experts is not good sense; it is. But pray beforehand that God will reveal his personal nudging to you. Perhaps that one thing that clicks and makes life easier. Perhaps one book's advice is good for now, but not good for later.

Maybe it doesn't apply at all to your lifestyle. Keep praying and listening for answers; confirm your course on a regular basis.

What would have happened to Isaac if Abraham had decided to stop listening after God told him to sacrifice his only son? What if he just concentrated on the altar and the knife, not hearing the next instruction God gave him? The one that said, "Do not lay a hand on the boy" (Gen 22:12).

Abraham did not have to sacrifice his son. He only had to show God he was *willing* to listen and obey. Stubborn mindsets can be lethal. Sometimes we do the right thing but carry on a little too long. Sometimes we do the wrong thing and pride keeps us from admitting it. Your children are watching! Ask God what to do next; be willing to listen and obey.

* * *

George and I were going through a particularly difficult time with Bret right after the broken-thumb incident. My back-yard ponderings were right on target: adolescence requires about a 9.9 on the Richter scale of tolerance. Finding the right balance between allowing him room to grow (i.e., be an adolescent jerk sometimes) and keeping him in line, seemed an impossible task short of pulling out all the hairs on our heads—one at a time.

We needed suggestions and direction. We needed to know that other parents were struggling with some of the same things we were, that our trauma (and progressing baldness) was normal and should be expected.

So we signed up for a one-day workshop I saw advertised in the local paper. I honestly can't remember who was sponsoring it, but it offered all kinds of rotating classes to choose from, and several seemed to headline our concerns.

Patiently we waited for the first speaker to arrive. She finally slunk in several minutes late, looking slightly frazzled.

"I'm sorry I'm late," she apologized. "I spent most of the night bailing my teenage son out of jail."

Our chorus of gasping was partly sympathetic and partly suspicious: *this* was the expert who was going to provide us with all the answers?

She went on to explain the circumstances. The incident wasn't nearly as bad as we imagined; no charges were pressed and her son had certainly learned a valuable lesson about the parties he should choose. There was also a lesson for us: even the experts cannot depend on their "expertness" when it comes to rearing perfect children!

Decisions come in all sizes; some are more major than others. Sometimes the same dilemma can seem like nothing one day and all consuming the next.

Take the issues of pacifiers and thumb sucking. Bret never did suck his thumb—basically, his hands were not idle long enough to take root in his mouth—but he used a pacifier for about a year. One day we lost the pacifier, and that was the end of that.

Brian, however, did them all. I made sure I had a pacifier on hand before I even brought him home from the hospital. Although I had made the decision to nurse him—something that appeared to be so natural yet sure took a lot of emergency phone calls to LaLeche League mothers—I just wanted to make sure there was something to put in his mouth should my chest not be within reasonable reach.

I found the pacifier to be a wonderful thing. When he would awaken in the middle of the night, he would, for just long enough, accept the pacifier while I changed him before I nursed. It kept him peaceful and let everyone else sleep; it allowed me to put him right down after he'd nursed and fallen asleep; it worked very well. Until he would lose his pacifier. So we bought several.

There are many who disagree with pacifiers. By the time Brian was three months old, so did he. One morning I peeked in on him and the pacifier was spit aside; his thumb was doing the job very nicely, thank you very much. His little fingers were circled around the satin edge of his blue blanket, forever transforming it to "blankie." Thus started a new chapter in our lives: Will Thumb Sucking Do Something Awful to Our Son? My friend Mary Beth said she sent up a flare when her daughter "finally found her thumb and could calm herself down." Others, however, tell frightful stories about buck teeth wicked enough to scrape wallpaper off the walls. Whatever, it all became an immaterial debate in our house because there was no getting that thumb out of Brian's mouth until he entered kindergarten.

The only good thing was that he could not suck his thumb unless he had blankie in his hand. He developed a certain style, the way all thumb suckers do. He would hold the corner in his right hand while sucking his right thumb. He would rub—and sniff—the very corner of blankie under his nose. No blankie, no thumb sucking.

When he was very young I could watch an upset baby immediately be calmed by the magic of his blankie and thumb. As he grew older, sometimes he would be playing and suddenly need a fix. He would cross the room to where the usually dirty blankie was slung over the side of a chair or bundled up in the corner, grab it, take a few drags, and off he'd go. I longed for a blankie in my own life.

I especially longed for one the year Bret had three automobile wrecks in six months. No one was hurt, thank the Lord, but needless to say all our insurance was cancelled. I also could have used one the day Brian came home his freshman year in high school and told me he wanted to wrestle.

"Gross! Isn't that the sport where you put your nose in someone's armpit?" I wanted to respond. But I didn't. I rode the beast bareback and hung on for dear life. I arranged a smile on my face and encouraged him to pursue his heart's desire.

He would come home after practice with mat burns on his forehead and I would listen to every grisly detail he unfolded about "take downs," "reversals," "pins," and the dreaded upcoming "challenge match." It was like a foreign language. All I understood was that he was very sore when he came home at night.

How much sympathy should a good parent give? Would it be too much like babying him? Should I admire the battle scars? Should I cheer or groan when he tells me he's won the challenge match, and that means I actually have to go watch him do this . . . this . . . thing. A noise uncontrollably escapes my mouth, not a cheer, not a groan, a sigh-like sound somewhere in between the two.

The entire day of the first meet I had heart palpitations picturing my little darling plastered to a sweat-beaded mat, wondering how I would ever encourage him to continue. (Oh for a blue blankie!) I watched the boys in the six-minute match before Brian's wrestle themselves into exhaustion. I didn't breathe. I practically twisted my husband's arm out of its socket. I didn't have a clue as to what all the ref's spasmodic gestures were about. Points had gone on the scoreboard and I didn't know why. (Was I too old to start sucking my thumb?)

When I saw Brian enter that ring wearing the headgear, breathing so heavily, I thought I was going to toss my cookies. He looked so vulnerable yet so brave. I was hyperventilating as he and his opponent shook hands. It was slow-motion torture. I moved his every

51

move. I felt his every mat burn. Strong against clever. Smart against quick. No room for the theatrics of channel 60 "profession-al" wrestlers here. Drop your concentration for a moment, and a near victory could bring swift defeat.

Brian lost that first match. But his determination and love for the sport grew. He developed a mutual liking with the coach who encouraged him and praised him with things like, "Baumbich, I think you've got a bubble in your butt because you always rise to the top." A very good thing in wrestling, believe it or not.

Watching the sport continued to be difficult for me—for all four years of high school. But I came to realize how much it meant to him, and how many lessons he was learning through this peculiar event: humility, perseverance, concentration, acceptance of self.

As the weeks went on, I cheered his every win and cheered his every loss. One on one. No one else to blame it on. No one else to share the win. All *his,* no matter what. I started looking forward to meets, and respected every single boy who took to the mats, no matter what school he was from.

I watched my son teach me many lessons about guts and sports-manship. We both learned to overcome first appearances: many are stronger than they look; bigger does not always mean better; yes, sometimes your nose ends up in an armpit, but there's nothing gross about triumph, respect for the opponent, or learning how to handle loss, even when your back is flat to the mat.

Over all, Brian had a successful high-school wrestling career, and his mother learned a lot about toughing it out too. But first, re-member, I had to dare to ride that beast bareback and hang on for dear life.

*   *   *

It's comforting to remember the Noah's ark story. God told Noah what to do. Noah did it. He didn't worry about who was going to close the door after he got all those animals on board. It's one of my favorite Scripture passages: "and the Lord closed it [the door] behind him" (Gen 7:16 NASB). The rest is history.

So pray, do what you think is best, double back when you realize an error, keep listening, and don't fret about the final outcome. God will close the door—or open it, or crack it a hair. Just pay attention so you don't miss it because you're blinded by your own fear and inadequacies.

The apostle Paul tells the believers, in Philippians 1:6, that he is "confident . . . that he who began a good work in you will carry it on to completion until the day of Christ Jesus." The Lord began two "good works" in me: Bret and Brian. And with them he also began the good work of making me a parent. A parent capable of passing on his blessings. And just think, it's his job to perfect it all. Yea, God!

•

**Dear Ex-Boss,
I can't come back to work;
my children need me.
Besides, I have a set of keys
to all my neighbors' houses
because I'm the only one
they know would be
home should they
lock themselves out.**

•

Four

Why I Can't Go Back to Work

Validation for Stay-at-Homes

"Keepers of the Big Wheel Brigade." *A title justly earned by Mary* Gingell and myself one summer when her son Noah and my Brian were about three. It wasn't the only title we bore, nor the grandest, I suppose, but nevertheless we wore it proudly.

Mary, Hugh and their two children lived right across the street from us—a blessing I continue to thank God for. Although we have lived far away from one another for many years now, when we do have occasion to get together, it is like we've never been apart. We bask in the familiarity of each other, never having to explain whence we've come. I do believe that women who have survived preschoolers together form an unbreakable bond.

I can picture us vividly. Mary's Dr. Scholl's sandals clip-clopping along Gingells' blacktop driveway. Noah's pants that simply did not ever stay slung above the top of the crease in his slimmer-than-slim buttocks. Brian always, but always, wearing a baseball cap with his ears tucked inside. He also hiked his pants up a little too high and wore his belts a little too tight—a habit, thank goodness, which he outgrew before the word "geek" came along. And me, well, I usually had a dish towel thrown over my shoulder and Mary had to remind me about it.

In retrospect, the fact that part of my "mommy" uniform was a dish towel was peculiar. During those busy years I honestly did not see the point in washing dishes that often, nor did I own a dishwasher. All everybody did was dirty them again. So I let them stack up into fairly large piles sometimes. There were just more important (or fun) things to do. By some mystery, however, the dish towel managed to ride my shoulder.

Anyway, that summer Mary and Hugh built a spacious, six-inch high deck right outside their front door and stained it red. Although that sounds a little peculiar—not the red but the six inches—it totally changed the atmosphere: we parked our lawn chairs on the deck instead of the blacktop driveway.

We spent a portion of almost every day on that deck watching the boys careen their Big Wheels at very high speeds toward the front end of the driveway, slam on the brakes, do a donut and roar back toward us—memories number 5,003 through 6,003. We experienced this racing duo at Gingells' house because our driveway was gravel and there were no sidewalks.

Day after day, time after time, Mary and I would take turns stopping our chatter mid-sentence to lunge after one of the boys who simply could not remember we told them NOT TO DRIVE TOO CLOSE TO THE STREET! I'm talking weeks of launching ourselves. Actually months.

Although it probably wasn't bad for our cardiovascular systems, the electrifying zap that rushes through a mother when she fears her child could meet with peril before she can reach him surely could be stroke-inducing. But we endured and even managed to solve world problems, as well as catch a few rays, between launches.

Then one day, life as we knew it was altered in a flash. A flash of inspiration. One of us, and I honestly can't remember who (but I hope it was me) was struck with a revelation: it was possible for us to sit at the front end of the driveway, thereby eliminating the need to live like astronauts.

We were stunned! It was so simple. So obvious. What took us so long to figure it out? Were we brain dead from being out of the working world so long?

No, we finally determined; we'd heard our husbands talk about plenty of business-world bloopers. In fact, we had each encountered doses of "business bonkers" in our own working-for-money worlds before children. So, after hashing it over a while we decided to give ourselves a break and celebrate our new and more relaxed lifestyle with giant ice teas and Popsicles all around.

*   *   *

That night as I lay in bed reading—husband dozing on the couch, boys long tucked in—something about the day gnawed at me. Not the discovery; it was grand, indeed. But our initial reaction to it.

After all, we were each committed to our choice. Content. Fulfilled. Convinced that our children deserved the best we could give them, and that was us. Happy to be free of corporate claws. Single-minded about our role. Grateful to be in a financial position that enabled us to stay home. Involved in clubs, crafts and miscellaneous volunteer projects that kept us sharp and well-rounded. So where did that reaction come from?

Other voices. Other voices that were starting to speak loudly about that time. A feminist movement that seemed to swing against some women, and eventually induced those women to start swinging back. There is nearly a full-fledged war going on now between many stay-at-home moms and career moms, and it grieves me deeply.

Who are we to judge one another when God specifically tells us time and again in the Scriptures that judgment is his job? How can we possibly know God's plan for another's life when we so often haven't a clue about our own? And why do we forget that the operative word here is "moms"? It is a title career moms and stay-at-home moms wear together.

Aren't we all just trying to do the best we can? Arming our children to enable them to fight the lures of today's world takes energy enough. Fighting each other is like clubbing your own team—and family. Who will win then? Certainly not the children who are left stranded on the bases while stay-at-homes balk at running interference for the career mom who can't take a turn in the car pool, and career moms demean the stay-at-homes, lowering their self-esteem. The children are stationed on the battlefield while we sling the mud.

Because I've walked in both sets of shoes—and believe me, neither of them walks an easy path—I'd like to present a little of each in hopes that each group may gain some insight into the other's role. The main thing is: the children need us, and we need each other.

I'll start this chapter by waving the apron, so to speak, for the home team because that is where my heart lies. But stay with me, working moms; the next chapter's for you.

When George and I married we talked about all the opportunities and options that were available to us. George lovingly took over the daily fathering responsibilities for Bret, the four-year-old son I brought into the marriage. There was no doubt in my mind that I had missed much of Bret in his early years as his natural father and I struggled to make ends meet while trying to hold together a failing relationship. Bret's and my difficult years continued alone for two years after the divorce.

Yes, there was no question that he needed more of me now, especially as we were entering a new marriage. It was a scary time for him.

George and I were also in total agreement that motherhood was a full-time job, and we wanted more children. I welcomed the opportunity to give concentrated energy to setting up a new nest. I filed myself in the ranks of the stay-at-homes and it came naturally to me.

My parents lived what used to be considered the "traditional roles." Dad went to work. Hammered and nailed things around the house. Coached little league, including my all-girl softball team. He was viewed as the great protector. He enjoyed relaxing with his family and always had a hug ready and waiting.

Mom worked at home: laundry, gardening, hanging clothes on the line, cooking, baking, taxiing her kids around, applying bandages, listening, sitting poolside while her kids screamed "Watch this!" from the top of the high dive. She laughed a lot and brimmed with passion for her family.

Traditional, familiar roles. I was relieved to be where I believed with all my heart that I belonged. I slipped right into my homemaker role with an audible sigh.

It didn't take long after Brian was born before the reality of how much I'd missed with Bret started soaking in. Now I could literally spend hours if I chose coaxing smiles from a three-month-old and receiving them. Nurturing security. Dinner didn't have to be "What can I throw together quick?" although I had that option and sometimes used it, but there was time to slowly simmer and baste. Create. Eat cookie dough.

I didn't have to wonder if Bret had his hat or not. I tugged it on his head, tied the muffler around his chin and started warming the hot chocolate.

When one is caught up in survival, one doesn't have time to mourn or even be aware of what isn't happening. Sometimes only from a distance can one step back and see the broad picture—filled with holes. And now I could clearly see that Bret's young life definitely held some buckshot.

I could not re-do Bret's early years, but I could begin that very moment basking in gratefulness that I was able to start experiencing and capturing the every-day miracles children deliver.

Don't get me wrong, all was not bliss. I also received healthy doses of scut work and crazy-making. Perhaps that's why passing through the "Big-Wheel-stay-at-home-mom" self-evaluation tripped me for a moment. Maybe life should be more than this, I said to myself. Maybe I was wrong to set aside career goals. Certainly life would be a lot easier with two incomes: I wouldn't have to darn socks just because a big toe escapes; I could throw them away and buy more! I wouldn't have to explain to Bret why he had to wear neat but rather generic jeans instead of the trendiest expensive ones. I wouldn't have to be catapulting myself out of a lawn chair days on end!

But those fleeting thoughts didn't last very long as I reflected once again on why I had chosen to stay home in the first place. I wanted to know my kids. Really *know my kids*. Develop a relationship with them.

Be there when they cried for me.

Witness unrepeated first steps. Oh sure, there are always other steps, endless other steps, but never those first ones again. And taking advantage of the opportunity to stay at home upped the odds that I would be in the right place at the right time to witness all those first and perhaps one-time-only accomplishments.

"Things happen so quickly," an acquaintance of mine once said, "that if you don't just sit still and look at them, you miss them." Amen. I valued the opportunity to give my children what my mother had given me; hours on end of undivided time.

One of my mother's tasks was ironing. I loved it when she ironed; she was a captive audience for my absolutely necessary and always urgent conversations. She would sip ice tea from her sweat-coated glass, then look into my eyes and search my face—maybe brush my hair away from my forehead—while I told the "really good stuff." Then she'd tackle the arm of a shirt or the crease in a pair of pants, ponder the magnitude of my trials and tribulations—or just sometimes the funny stuff—and respond with head nods and verbal acknowledgments. The iron would hiss when it hit the sprinkled clothes, and I would feel as warm as the ironed sleeve because my mother was listening, really listening. That's what I wanted to do for my children.

I also wanted to hang clothes out on the line, and I had the time to do it, weather permitting. Relaxing on a breezy day, watching sheets flap and snap, gathering them in my arms and inhaling the universe . . . I could monitor the boys while they ran through the sprinkler, could laugh at their playfulness and at the same time capture peace with clothespins. I viewed it as part of my responsibility to keep the Norman Rockwell image of life at home alive and well.

Mom had let my brother and me absolutely destroy her kitchen with wild concoctions. Baking. Experimenting. Testing the way food colors mixed with powdered sugar; rolling out home-made egg noodle dough—and then eating all the noodles before they dried. And so, too, my children would have this opportunity for leisurely play. Creativity boosters. After all, the child in me loved an excuse for this behavior as well. Still does. My husband and boys wouldn't have recognized Thanksgiving as a holiday if noodles weren't strung around the kitchen to dry, disappearing one by one each time one of us passed through.

And messes can always be cleaned up. In fact, they present opportunities for character building and responsibility.

Some of the best days I shared with my kids were the ones which had absolutely no plans in them. We would wake up in the morning with no place to go. No shopping to do. An entire day before us to spend time together. Or alone—each in our own corner with nothing rushing us out. Unhurried time. Time for couch cushions to become walls to forts. Time for Legos to transport them to Mars and me into a quiet time zone in which to read.

* * *

One mother told me how she simply enjoyed watching her children play together. She had been an only child, and spoke of the loneliness that sometimes surrounded her as she grew up. She said she cherished the moments her children shared with each other. Oh sure, sometimes they bickered, but she knew the bond between them was much stronger than the antagonism.

Another stay-at-home mom, who referred to herself as somewhat crafty, enjoyed the opportunity to share in that with her daughter. Although her daughter is not yet four, she has shared enough cut-out time with mom to warrant her own set of "good" scissors that don't mutilate the paper. She even clips coupons for mom with them. And together they organize and plan.

Even wallpapering became fair game for sharing in one family. "I gave them their own pan of wallpaper paste," the mother boasted. I don't think I would have had the courage to do that, but Brian often pulled up a chair next to me if I was working at the kitchen sink. I would be chopping and dicing and he would be filling the sink with water and floating things in it. Or helping me dry. Or watching the squirrels play in the back yard, right by my side.

Bret, Brian and I had time not only to smell the flowers together but to plant them as well. There was time to read them stories as they cuddled in my lap. Or sat next to me, making up their own stories as they saw fit. Children who are just learning how to talk are wonderful entertainers, and how better to get them to vocalize than by being their audience. Honestly, their stories can be a lot more interesting than any soap opera.

As the children grew older, I found it even more important to be home when they busted in through the front door. Bigger kids have bigger problems and more options of places to seek solutions. I wanted that chance to hear all about it and give my input before they found another way—a scarier way—to struggle through it besides sharing it with family.

I was available to help other mothers' children as well, many working moms' children, and that was a blessing to me. Emergency runs to school for those who missed their bus after Mom or Dad left. Picking up another's sick child from school and holding a hand until a worried parent could make it home from work. Room mother. Field-trip chaperone. All duties I enjoyed and found fulfilling.

Of course, I did get scratched off one volunteer list due to an unfortunate accident. I made cupcakes for hot dog day at the grammar school. How was I to know a screw had fallen out of my mixer into the batter? I didn't *mean* for it to show up in the little boy's mouth right behind the chocolate frosting.

Before I start sounding like I believe that simply staying home with your children solves all the problems, let me set the record straight: it does not. That assumption is far from the truth. Stay-at-homes and their children can fall victim to all kinds of dangers, pitfalls and lures.

Let's start with compulsion and overindulgence. The kind of relationship with your children that can make other people want to smack you and scream, "Get a life!" The kind that smothers and oppresses and stifles the very things in our children we are trying to nurture. The kind that exhausts—both us and our children.

When you have nothing in your life but your kids, tunnel vision can encompass you. It can sneak up on you. Consume you. Leave you an empty, lifeless shell when they are gone. Full-time parents must strive for balance. Learn to see beyond the family room so they can introduce their children to the rest of the world.

We can strive so hard to be good, twenty-four-hour-a-day parents that we become confused and blind to simple reality. Children are no longer a blessing to behold and celebrate; they have become a job. A job we take so seriously and neurotically that we cannot see the truth through the facts: Yes, children are work, but they are joy and life and creativity and spontaneity and pleasure. We can be looking so hard at each little element of their lives that we miss the whole of who they are, who they are becoming.

We need to guard against losing ourselves in our children; otherwise, who will they turn to in times of trouble if we are no longer our own strong selves but rather a part of them?

I can still fall victim to compulsive "steering" occasionally, even though my boys are young men. While they are away from me, whether permanently living away or just at college for the school year, I am forced to let go, turn them out to pasture—just as working parents are forced to do during the day. Independence creates room to grow, for all parties concerned.

*   *   *

But the temptation to ride that horse with spurs the minute it's back within reach doesn't really go away. If you've become rusty at dealing with the temptation, or let your guard down, ZAP! It's got you!

I remember the first time Bret came home for a brief visit after he'd graduated and moved to Albuquerque. I busied myself for days getting everything just perfect. I even cleaned both bathrooms and (egads!) the silverware drawer.

I set aside the rest of my life for this visit. After all, he hadn't been home for fourteen months and I was overflowing with anticipation. I planned meals and pictured us sitting around talking and talking. Doing things together. Mother and son. Yucking it up and catching lunch and. . . .

Sure, those things happened, but not twenty-four hours a day. He had friends to see and places to go and ground to cover, as well he should have. I hadn't raised a slug or a hermit; what did I expect?

I became snappy and clingy and a royal pain; there's simply no way to soften the description of my behavior. I strongly suggested who he might want to call and what he might like to do with them. Then I started laying guilt trips on him because he wasn't checking in and out with me before his every move, and on and on and on.

I had set myself up to fall in the trap. My need to know I was still important in his life—although he had never given me cause to doubt it—caused me to slip gears and engage in an obsessive, overbearing, "Get-a-life!" mode.

It happens just as easily when they're young. Yes, they need you to cross the street. But they don't need you to tell them where to sit in the sandbox and whom they should invite to sit in there with them—like you, for instance.

The flip side of this behavior: the parents who choose not to work outside the home but don't stay home or pay much attention to their kids either. They're easy to spot. They've got the kids enrolled in every activity in the world and they spend most of their time dropping them off, picking them up—trying to mold and shape their children's lives by seeing they are exposed to everything. Everything but time to play with Mom and Dad. Sit. Ponder. Explore. Cuddle in their laps.

These parents honestly believe they are over-taxed and their conversations are filled with martyristic mumblings. Or they are full of boasting about all the skills their children are mastering; yet all their children really want to accomplish is getting Mom's or Dad's attention. Undivided. Not because of what they are achieving, but simply because of who they are: a fragile child.

It is easy to fall into Super Parent behavior. Room mother, Brownie leader, Sunday-school teacher—a mother to everyone's child but your own.

There are non-working mothers who spend as much time volunteering, working out, watching television and gallivanting around as their working-mom counterparts spend on the job. Just saying you're a stay-at-home doesn't make it so.

Balance. Every mom needs to find balance.

Yes, basically I rally on the side of the stay-at-home. That's because I felt so fulfilled being there, and I knew that one day, the rest of my life would resume. And so it has, with great vigor.

I shall always cherish those at-home years. As crazy as it sounds, even my two-year stint as Bret's den mother was incredibly rewarding. It was amazing how many creative outlets that offered: ingenuity, planning for every minute so you didn't lose control of the rowdy group, reacting quickly to brewing difficulties, channeling the energy of the boys. We had one of the happening-est dens in the pack, and all of us were very proud of that.

Oh sure, den mothering had its down sides too. Like the time I almost wiped out one of the eight-year-olds when we were preparing for the "Christmas around the World" pack meeting. I had him doing a dance on a Mexican sombrero—something, it turns out, he was outrageously allergic to. Severe hives consumed him within minutes.

And then there's the time the group as a whole—excluding me or my permission, of course—decided to find out just how gross it would be if they could all (eight boys) pass gas at the same time in my basement. That almost snuffed all of us out.

But on the whole, fond Cub Scout memories are captured forever. As are the days the boys and I went on spontaneous picnics or off to the zoo or Kiddieland. Kool-Aid went down by the gallon. Summer days were, in general, lazy and relaxing. Winter brought snow angels and awesome forts.

I have a picture of my boys standing next to an outhouse at one of the county parks we visited on a brisk fall day. They are standing on a blanket of leaves, one on each side of the sign that reads "Men." They are flexing their skinny little four- and ten-year-old bodies to the max, trying to live up to the sign.

And now they are men. And now they are gone. And I usher them back with full-bloomed stay-at-home memories. And I am thankful and proud to be a mother who, most of the time, enjoyed her life as an apron waver—even though sometimes it looked suspiciously like a white flag.

•

Dear Son,

Thanks for making the

wonderful centerpiece that

adorned our dinner

table tonight. Your superb

placement of three matchbox cars

and a robot was exquisite.

•

· Five ·

Loosening the Straitjacket

Permission for Working Moms

It's 5:10 p.m. and I'm just heading out the office door. The day-care lady's going to have my hide . . . again. But worse than that, Bret's face is going to be a mile long. He will be among the last couple of children left waiting by the door to be rescued.

I dread the guilt that is already swallowing me. Not just because I'm late, but because Bret doesn't much care for the center anyway—to put it mildly. His little three-year-old voice asks me every day if he has to go. It's affordable, it had an opening, it's on the route between work and the apartment, it's my only choice in the matter.

"Yes, son, you must go." Every day I hate telling him that. Every day he hates hearing it. Yet we each go through the motions without applying the brakes. We each do what we must.

As a perker-upper for both of us, while he pulls on his coat I tell him we'll stop on the way home at McDonald's. This doesn't elicit much response; McDonald's is becoming old hat. We stop there anyway and get carry-out. The fragrance of fries wafts up to our hungry noses. We decide to sneak a few from the bag while we sit in rush-hour traffic.

Halloween decorations are beginning to pop up around the neighborhood. He tells me there's going to be a party at school. We speculate as to what the costume of choice might be: Dracula, ghost and clown are touched on. We are both glad for the distracting thoughts, yet the conversation is not a lively one.

Upon arriving home we unwrap our burgers and dump the fries out on the edge of our makeshift plates. I grab the ketchup and pour a couple glasses of milk. We sit in the dim light of the kitchen and eat in silence. We are both exhausted.

Bret plays in the bathtub for a while. I turn on the television and try to unwind as I pick up the morning's mess left behind. Bret soon calls for me to come wrap him up in a towel. We get his "jammies" on and watch a little television together. I tuck him in. I'm not far behind; morning swings around in a hurry. Another day is chalked off our calendars.

The pattern repeats with only slight variations from day to day. Halloween draws near. A clown it will be. We have most of the makings to whip that up; cheap is always in order.

The night before the party we take the old red pillow case with white polka dots (where in the world that thing came from I have no earthly idea) and cut a head hole and two arm holes in it. I have an old white feather hair net left over from the big fad in the sixties; we decide to use it as a headpiece. Early the next morning, I spend a considerable amount of time applying my version of clown makeup: white base, lipstick around his eyes and mouth, green eye shadow here and there. Voila! A clown.

Bret takes one look in the mirror and hates it. He's not going as a clown! he declares.

"There is no time for anything else!" I reply. "Besides, you look great," I say, and I mean it. I do not convince him. He begins to cry and the makeup runs. I fuss around, making funny faces, trying to get the gist of what's wrong. He is utterly sad and I don't know why.

He will not, cannot, stop crying. This is not like him. He's always been busy and rambunctious; he has never been a crybaby. In fact, rarely does he cry. He was blessed with a chipper personality and the ability to overcome or simply grind on through the tough stuff.

But now he cries. From the depth of him, he cries. For the life of me, I do not, cannot understand what it's all about. The clock is ticking. It's time to leave for work.

I run and grab the camera to capture this little clown on film, hoping some coaxing antics will cheer him up. He has always been a ham for the camera. It does not cheer him up. I still have the picture of that little elfin face, tears mixed with white makeup around his chin. Fresh ones brimming out of his deep brown eyes over his thick, long lower lashes.

After a near all-out power struggle—not physical, but commanding—finally I drop him off at school. He is slump-shouldered and holding back another flood. He is still dressed as a clown and hating it. I kiss him good-bye and bid him to have a good time. The door closes behind me. I cry all the way to work. I cry once more as I write this story that is twenty-three years in my past.

*   *   *

This scene has never blurred or softened at the edges in my memory portfolio. It is one of those time periods I would like to do over but cannot. Today, Bret says he can't remember what the tears were all about; I am grateful for that. But he knows it happened because he's seen the photograph many times.

I believe it has vividly stuck in my mind for a couple of reasons. It was symbolic of many things that were wrong with our lives during that time. I honestly believe Bret's tears overflowed from a very deep well having nothing to do with clowns and everything to do with time, or lack of. That vivid image serves as a reminder of how easily we can miss our kids, because certainly I was, unintentionally, robbing both of us. Not because I was working, although there is no getting around the fact that work robs our children of time with us, but because I had not yet realized a few valuable lessons.

I hadn't learned to stand my ground. I hadn't realized the importance of sticking to priorities. And I hadn't given myself permission to play. Fortunately for both of us, the clown incident triggered a good long search for what was wrong.

Gradually I figured out some very important things—and I believe the Lord used them to help me make some basic attitude changes.

STAND YOUR GROUND. Lessons on standing my ground came in bundles and made life much easier once they became ingrained through practice. I needed to be firm with my workplace and myself. These lessons also apply to stay-at-home moms who find themselves slaves to volunteer work and other over-extended commitments. Here's what I learned:

Five o'clock p.m. meant go get my son. Immediately. Not after I'd jotted one more thing down or passed on one more message or dropped something in the mailbox. It meant watch the clock and start winding down ten minutes earlier. It meant not answering the phone at the stroke of five. It meant eliminating the guilt of being late. It meant no more evenings started with long faces. It meant the gaining of trust and security for and from my son. It meant GO HOME. Amazingly, life at work did not fall apart when I started this practice. Being the last one out the door, I realized, had not proven my loyalty or won me an award or more money. It simply meant I had gotten sloppy with my time somewhere along the way and set the stage for anxiety.

STICK TO YOUR PRIORITIES. "No way do I waste ten minutes in my day!" you say. Monitor yourself, then try it. There's an old saying: work expands to meet the time allotted to it. Exactly. Do not allot tardy. Ten minutes a day, five days a week borders on an hour of stress-inducing time that can be cut from your life. It doesn't matter if you are the husband or wife, mommy or daddy, you and your family deserve this respect.

Prioritize those ten minutes, or whatever your personal goal time is. Maybe you are a punctual person, but try using the car trip or the train ride home for the same purpose. Whatever, see that block of time as an opportunity to call forth a thankful spirit that this part of the day is behind you and a cherished portion is beginning.

Don't groan; give me a chance here. Remind yourself that you are going home to a precious gift. God's gift to you. Granted, this takes serious work some days! And sometimes you do your part, but then you get home and your child behaves very unlike a cherished gift! My friend Mary Beth uses a phrase during times when one of her children is being obnoxious that has really stuck with me. She audibly refers to the troublesome child as "Oh Child of God." What an awesome reminder!

PERMISSION TO PLAY. Shock yourself daily with the following announcement to your attitude: you have permission to look forward to embracing, gaining pleasure from and playing with your children.

It is oh so easy to take your tired work self and let it fall into the trap of just going through the motions. Look for opportunities for creative relaxation and enjoyment. Maybe you won't find them every time—but then again, maybe you will.

*　　*　　*

I remember another evening not long after the clown episode. I'm out the door at the stroke of five, talking to my attitude all the way to the day-care center—or nursery school, as they were referred to back then. Work has been very harried. I choose a classical music channel, as opposed to depressing news, and consciously free my mind, then begin picturing Bret's small frame waiting, needing to be hugged, just as I do. I ponder the fact that perhaps his day hasn't been so hot either.

He is very happy to see me. The hug says it all.

Bret and I sit in traffic; I tell him the good and bad parts about my day. He, in turn, shares some of his. We decide we deserve something special. It is simply time for the horses to graze in fresh pastures. Even a bareback rider would be too much weight this day. And so, a quick run through the supermarket turns up a package of those crackers that come with the cheese that you spread with a stick, a fresh box of raisins, a bag of carrots and two push-up ice cream bars.

Bret stands on a chair pulled up to the sink next to me. He peels the carrots; I cut them into strips; he plunks them in a glass of ice water. I remove the covers from the cheese packets; he places things on the table. I ask him to create a centerpiece while I get a candle. Just because I've never seen three matchbox cars and a robot used for a centerpiece doesn't mean it can't be done, and so it is. I pour the glasses of milk. He sprinkles some raisins on our paper plates. The candle is lit and we unwind, share and laugh together.

He plays in the tub for a while. I clean up the mess left behind from the morning rush. We eat our orange push-ups on a pink blanket in the middle of the blue living room, sitting cross-legged on the floor. I read him a story and we talk about Valentine's Day which is still about three weeks off.

I have spent a good deal of time lately trying to remember the utter importance special holidays hold for children. I think of bareback riding and anticipate a corner, leaning into it for balance. I certainly don't want to get trampled like I did Halloween. We decide to stop on the way home tomorrow evening and buy some red construction paper and paper doilies. We already have plenty of glue. There are a few people I would like to send some cards to also. I'll make mine as well. Why not?

Bret goes to bed. I'm not far behind. I must get up extra early and throw a load of clothes in the washer so I can hang them around the bathroom before we leave in the morning. Although there is much to do, peace surrounds me as I close my eyes.

Not all days after my "awakening" were like this. But more were close to it than were not. I certainly wasn't June Cleaver and Bret wasn't the Beav. There was no Ward in our home at the time. We lived in the real world. But my attitude had changed, and therefore, so had I.

*   *   *

I was discussing this whole topic recently with a close friend of mine who happens to be a social worker. She agreed that attitude can do amazing things. Then she reminded me that one has to be equipped with a reserve to dip into, in order to be able to pull out that good attitude, and sometimes we just don't have reserve.

Point well taken. It's true. We earthly humans can flat out run dry. But God never does, and he is the one who fills us up with the Holy Spirit, the Counselor, the Comforter—the healing Attitude-Changer. That's why it's so important for us to give him our reins before we come to the end of ourselves. He will lead us to, and fill us with, refreshing waters (Ps 23:2). He promises us that if we drink of the water he gives us, we will never thirst (Jn 4:13-14).

"Let us then approach the throne of grace with confidence, so that we may receive mercy and find grace to help us in our time of need," Hebrews 4:16 reads. Draw near. Drink. Mercy. Grace. Blessing upon blessing. There for the taking.

And keep this in mind when you are fretting—it's something my dad has said to me since I was small. It's amazing how many times it rings true—when I remember to let it. *Ten years from now it won't make a bit of difference. And maybe even tomorrow.*

* * *

It's something I wanted to say to a mother I never met—although my heart ached for her after I heard about her child, whom I also never met. I was reporting a story for a newspaper, a story about lunchroom behavior from pre-school through college. How do kids decide who to sit with? What do they talk about? What social function does the lunch period serve? It was a light story and fun. I enjoyed talking to kids, lunchroom supervisors and teachers. Never did I expect to hear something so sad.

Perhaps it impacted me so strongly because I live across the street from a day-care center. Every morning I watch mothers and an occasional father drag sleepy children out of cars—sometimes not long after seven a.m. Some are carrying blankets and other pieces of their lives. Many don't get picked up until after six p.m. It settled me some to actually visit inside a facility and see that the children are well cared for.

But I heard a disturbing story that stuck with me. Day-care workers had to teach a child how to feed itself. A child far beyond the age when most children clumsily learn this task. It seems the mother was always in a hurry, as well as tired from all the rush, and so feeding the child herself saved her not only valuable time but mess.

I wanted to track down that poor mother and say, "Ten years from now the twenty minutes you saved each day escaping clean-up won't make a bit of difference to the success of your life, and maybe even tomorrow. But it certainly will to your child."

I wanted to give her permission to re-evaluate her system. I wanted her to have memories like I do. Memories of fat little fingers and palms spread out over a gaping mouth, trying to get the tasty morsels to stay where they belong. A crooked little plastic spoon that helps a toddler wield the tipsy load in the right direction. The triumphant grin that spreads across a munchkin's face when he has hunted down an escaped pea on his highchair tray, finally picks it up and now holds it between his toothless gums grinning like a baboon.

Yes, kids learning to eat create many a mess. Often they are intentional, as in the "bombs away" game they play leaning over the side of the high chair grinning, watching milk or handfuls of applesauce splat on the floor. But it is part of what we remember for the rest of our lives. It is another step toward their independence, which comes flying at us with the speed of the first downhill slope on a roller coaster.

Take time, find time, create time to enjoy your children. Cancel some of their lessons if you have to, or sign up for something with them. Watch them pick out their own clothes for the day and ask them why they made that choice. So what if they don't match? "Ten years from now. . . ."

Sometimes put out a towel for them next to your exercise mat and work out together instead of dropping them off or leaving them behind to go to your workout. You will have all the days of your life to exercise alone after they're gone.

Give yourself a mental break: no parent is doing it all and doing it well. Don't put unfair expectations on yourself. If another mother is doing her best to give you a guilt complex when you know, beyond the shadow of a doubt, that God has called you to do what you're doing, ask God to soften her heart, as well as yours.

"Each one should use whatever gift he has received to serve others, faithfully administering God's grace in its various forms" (1 Pet 4:10). Take heart in knowing that you are following God's plan for your life. Use your own gifts for your own family—and beyond. Don't envy or imitate somebody else. What you've got is *special.*

Stay-at-home moms need to be reminded that many working moms are tending to their children: schoolteachers, YMCA instructors, dance instructors, doctors and nurses, the lady at the dry cleaner's who got the spots out of the confirmation dress, the postal employee who delivers her child's letter to Grandma, waitresses, day-care workers (babysitters), the lady who cuts her child's hair just in time for school pictures, the editor of her child's Sunday-school literature . . . all helping, in one way or another, to care for her child.

A long-term friend of mine and I were recently conversing about where we are in our lives: both empty nesters, she is now an officer in a bank and I'm a very busy writer. Both careers began after the children were in high school. We are living proof of that old adage, "It's never too late."

But we don't have much time to get together anymore, and we were bemoaning that fact. When the kids were little, she, like Mary, was another bosom buddy with whom I spent a good deal of time. Her children were a few years older than mine and seemed to be doing fine, so she naturally became one of my mentors.

Now when we get together, after updating news of our families' progress and checking off our latest achievements, the conversation always rambles its way back to "the good old days," and we begin reminiscing about the tribulations and triumphs we shared while raising the "youngens."

During this particular visit recently, our conversation danced with anecdotes as vivid as neon jogging clothes. Our children were young, and we were young, and laughter, frustration, joy and tears spilled as often as the milk at the dinner table.

And then we started talking about today's too-busy parents and our mood swung to sad. Big houses, mounds of toys, several cars, climbing the corporate ladder, day care; tired parents, single parents, overdue bills, latchkey kids.

"All their children's memories will belong to someone else," she lamented. "They will be the treasures of whoever is watching their kids." We carried on this line of conversation for some time. It was easy for a judgmental tone to hover around our comments.

After I arrived home and reflected on our conversations, it occurred to me that I had a very short memory.

Visions of a weeping clown crept into my mind.

And then I realized that "all their children's memories will belong to someone else" isn't totally true. Yes, many will. And one hopes they're not first steps or first words or dance recitals and baseball games. But working parents can collect volumes of happy memories about and with their children, simply by giving themselves permission to have, and working at, a little creative, spontaneous enjoyment. Time to play. Warm memories.

Working parents will probably collect their own clown story somewhere along the way, too. But find me any parent without one and I'll show you somebody who's really missed their kids!

•

Dear God,
When you mirrored my
torqued-up face for me
today, I learned just how
silly Stubborn looks.
Who says you
don't have a sense of humor?

•

· Six ·

When All Else Fails, Laugh

Humor

I honestly believe that a sense of humor is as vital to joy-filled memories as a pacifier is to a screaming baby's mouth, and you already know how I feel about pacifiers.

I'd like to focus here on the importance—vital importance, healing importance, saving grace importance—of finding the funny side. And there is almost always a funny side. A ludicrous ("ludicrous" as defined in Webster's New World Dictionary: "laughably absurd") element that keeps the cannon from going off and enables you to move past the moment.

Sometimes the laughably absurd side of the situation doesn't hit you until much later, thereby transforming a traumatic encounter into a hilarious memory. Other times, a snicker erupts the instant your mind translates reality into . . . into . . . the laughably absurd.

If it happens on the spot, it can save the day.

For instance, when the apostle Peter said, "But do not forget this one thing, dear friends: With the Lord a day is like a thousand years, and a thousand years are like a day" (2 Pet 3:8), he was explaining that the Lord is not slow; God's time is not our time. He was giving us the long view. I suspect, however, that among his readers during those days there was at least one parent of a defiant teenager, grounded adolescent or baby with diarrhea who snickered out loud, then hollered, "Amen! You can say that again, Buster! One day is definitely like a thousand years!" I know I've had that thought many a time.

And I had one of those "days" when Brian was about two-and-one-half years old. By total grace, a parental victory prevailed at the conclusion of this particular incident, but it was a lion's den for sure—an arena I thankfully never had to enter again. A sense of humor ultimately—and accidentally—became the weapon that allowed me to survive the war.

Brian was in need of new shoes, and he hated anything new, including the mere suggestion.

*   *   *

"Guess what, Brian?" I say, as chipper as humanly possible.

"What!" he declares more than answers as he sits spellbound in front of the television while Bert and Ernie do their thing.

"Today's the day you get to pick out a brand new pair of shoes!"

"No. I don't want to."

"But Brian, you are getting to be such a big boy now. Your feet have grown so much your toes are touching the ends of your shoes."

"So?"

"So, we certainly don't want your toes to get crooked and start hurting."

"I don't care if they do."

"Well, I bet you're tired of looking at those worn out-old shoes. I know I am."

He takes the end of blankie that isn't trailing from his mouth and covers his shoes with it. "I don't look at them." He also doesn't look at me during any of this conversation.

"How about this? How about we get you a pair of gym shoes?" A daring suggestion since white, square-toed, leather high-top jobbies were about all anyone's child wore back then.

"No. NO NEW SHOES."

"But new gym shoes can run fast and jump high!"

"I CAN run fast. I don't want to jump high."

"You need them, Brian," I say through tightening lips.

"I don't want to go," he replies, just as tight.

"We have to go, Honey." I have read somewhere that using terms of endearment softens the listener—and the message. "It's not a matter of whether you want to go or not, Sweetheart. This is not a discussion. You have to go."

"I'm not going."

Okay, I say to myself, control yourself and think this through.

You can pick him up and carry him to the car and into the shoe store, kicking and screaming all the while. Or you can stall the excursion a bit until his mood turns more toward the agreeable.

You've got plenty of laundry you can start on, truckloads of ironing you can perhaps make a dent in, a bag of chocolate chips that are just waiting to become cookies. You can get those kinds of things behind you before you set out on a journey. And remember, we're talking riding bareback, not breaking wild broncos. There is time in this lovely spring day to find a peaceful solution.

I'm sure of it.

"Well, I don't want to go right now, anyway," I say rather too perkily. "We won't go until after lunch. Maybe we can get an ice cream cone for dessert on the way home from getting your new shoes."

Silence.

I translate this silence as a form of truce and agreement. Oh silly me.

By the time the peanut-butter-and-honey sandwich crumbs are being whisked off the table, I find myself trying to think of an invitation to buy new shoes that can't be refused, which seems a dichotomy in itself: What normal person doesn't like new shoes anyway? But, this is Brian, exactly as God gave him to us. Our gift to treasure and love—not necessary to understand. So on with the mental gymnastics.

The ice cream cone seed has already been planted; now how to get a mention of the shoes back in there without sounding an alarm? I do, however, want to make sure the ground rules are clearly understood before we depart on this SHOE-BUYING jour-ney. And from experience I know that the normally fun, happy and agreeable Brian has a way of digging in occasionally, to say the least. Digging himself in to the bottom of the miry pit. And today, he has already reached for the shovel.

And so, right or wrong, the challenge suddenly becomes: to use the gift of creative thinking God has given me to smooth the way and help save this kid from himself. After all, my goal is to raise a cooperative child, not an inferior subordinate.

"So, are you ready for an ice cream cone?" I ask.

"Not if I have to get shoes first."

"How about if we get the ice cream cone first?"

"Okay," he says flatly.

I smile and rumple the wispy blonde hair on top of his cute little strong-willed head. At this point in time there is nothing funny brewing. Nothing. War is in the air. My motherly intuition is sounding its alarm.

Our ice cream cones go down without incident. Like NASA, I feel the countdown begin. "T" minus a ten-second pause and counting. Nine, eight, seven . . . liftoff!

"Okay!" I say with a flurry of excitement. "Let's go get those new shoes!"

"I told you I'm not getting new shoes."

"Brian, you need new shoes and we are getting them today. We're leaving on vacation soon and this is the only chance we'll have." The excitement in my voice has dissipated for this announcement. It is replaced by an authoritative command. "You got your ice cream, now it's time to get your shoes. Get your fanny in the car! We're going to the shoe store. Now."

We throw our sticky, ice cream-residue napkins away and head for the car. The ride to the shoe store is not a long one—maybe five minutes—but seems to take an hour. I am busy making a plan for all the possibilities. But maybe I don't need one. He did get in the car, right?

Wrong. In my wildest dreams I could not have foreseen what was to transpire.

We park the car and he reluctantly dawdles his way into the shoe store. We browse around at the rather large display of children's shoes. No matter which one I suggest, he hates it. He hates them all. He doesn't want white. He doesn't like colors.

"They're dumb. They don't have any I like. Let's go home," he says. "I like my old ones."

War is past the brewing stage now. The trenches are dug, the warriors are prepared for battle. If ever I hate to be reminded of the stubborn bent I have, it is here and now. His squinted little brow mirrors mine. We stand facing each other with arms crossed in front of us.

"We're not leaving without new shoes," I say matter-of-factly. It takes every ounce of control I have to keep from throwing a major hissing fit. I muster this control, however, while I try to sort out my scrambled brain. I need a plan. A plan to make good on the announcement I just heard myself make.

I run through a battery of options:

(1) I can try to cram his foot into a shoe. I immediately rule this out because I don't have money to throw away on shoes that don't actually fit, and there will be no way to know this for sure without a good measure on cooperative toes.

(2) I can whisk him back to the car. No dice. He will have won: his "NO NEW SHOES!" announcement will have prevailed.

(3) I can spank him, causing submission. Nasty scene in a shoe store. Brian's reaction to a spanking is not usually one of submission. Isolation works best for him, but then we're back to #2 which I have already ruled out.

(4) I can admit I don't know what to do. Right.

But I do know that love is patient, and patience is a fruit of the Spirit.

I go with #4 because I truly don't know what else to do, and I hope that through patience I'll learn what to do. Exhausted sigh follows this decision.

Firmly I grip his sweet little arm and lift him into one of the chairs. Nose to nose I explain that it is time to get shoes.

He counters my oh-so-firm announcement by sitting on his feet.

This is *not* the point in the story where I see how humorous the situation is. Many things flash through my mind; laughter is not one of them. I grab two shoes off the display area, blow a hair off my forehead and settle in.

"Can I help you?" a salesman asks, looking directly at Brian.

"No."

"Yes," I quickly counter. "Brian needs new shoes."

"Okay, big guy, let's have a measure, here." The salesman reaches beneath the chair next to Brian and produces the familiar silver appliance. Brian stares at him and doesn't move. I try to remain calm.

"Okay, son, let's see that growing foot." The man touches Brian's knee. Brian breaks eye contact and doesn't respond.

"Why don't you give us a minute?" I say. "We seem to need a little adjusting time."

"Fine. Just give a holler when you're ready." He retreats to behind the counter where the cash register is and I see him talking to the female cashier. She laughs. I do not.

"Brian," I say through my teeth, "we are not leaving here until you get some new shoes. Why don't you just put your foot out there, let the man measure, pick out a shoe and we'll be done."

"No."

"Then we'll just sit here until you change your mind. I don't care if it takes all day." It occurs to me that it just might.

"Can I help you?" a young saleslady asks. I look at Brian. He doesn't look at me, or her.

"Not just yet," I chirp.

"Let me know if you need help," she says, and proceeds to huddle with the other two behind the counter.

Let her know if I need help? Isn't it obvious I need a miracle?

*   *   *

Brian and I continue to sit in silence for what seems like an eternity. This could take longer than I planned on, but it will finally happen, I reassure myself. In the meantime, I just need to have patience . . . patience . . . patience . . . patience to come up with a plan.

While I'm busy entertaining the idea of hanging myself with a 24″ shoelace from the display next to me (a plan I rule out as soon as I realize Brian still won't get any shoes), the salespeople smile at me as they pass by with armloads of boxes. Shoes other people and their children are buying. Some of them are getting more than one pair. Parents and their little darlings are chatting and laughing.

I am reminded of all the times laughter rings throughout our house. So much of it begins with Brian, too: his expressions, his natural bent to explore and the joy that comes with discovery, antics that delight and entertain, sweet and precious moments he gives us with kisses, hugs and uncommon stories. . . .

And then the original salesman interrupts my daydreaming by appearing before me. He doesn't speak, but he wears a look on his face that says, "Well, how about it? Are we ready now?"

I take one hopeful look at Brian and am slam-dunked out of the sounds of ringing laughter and back into reality. I shake my head in denial.

Minutes tick by. Brian's shins grow roots in the chair. Inner dialoguing runs rampant. Once a parent takes a stand, I silently tell myself, and after they have considered the rationale of the situation, if the original stand is correct, they should stick to it. That is the case here.

Waiting has become my plan.

Brian looks at me out of the corner of his eye and I swear he reads my mind. A couple more shovels of imaginary dirt can be seen flying over each of our shoulders as we dig our trenches a little deeper.

Brian has shifted several times but continues to harbor his feet under his buttocks. I'm sure his legs have fallen asleep and must be driving him nuts.

Suddenly, as he is mid-shift, I am swept with an overview of this ludicrous scene. My mind replays the laughably absurd day in its entirety and a laugh begins to rankle around in my throat. I make several attempts to swallow it down, but it bubbles and perks ever higher, until finally it erupts, startling the near-dozing Brian.

"What's so funny?" he asks.

"Oh, nothing. I was just thinking how silly it would be, sleeping here tonight. And if you'll excuse me, I need to make a couple phone calls. I've got to call Mrs. Gingell so she can let Bret know why no one will be home when he gets off the school bus. And I have to call Dad and tell him to go ahead and eat dinner on his way home, and to not expect us."

Brian's eyes nearly pop out of his head. I realize I'm on to something here. And so for good measure I add, "I'll tell Dad to bring us the sleeping bags and a flashlight. Bet it gets dark in here."

Brian says nothing. I, his mother, who has finally seen the humor in this war, sit next to him chuckling like a loony-tune. I thrash through my purse collecting change for the phone. "I'll be right back. Sit tight." I nearly lose control as this line slips out of my mouth. Like he needs a directive to do *that*? I'm hysterical. What a gas! "Sit tight," I repeat through waves of laughter. "Isn't that funny?"

Suddenly, one of Brian's legs slips out from under him. He cringes at the pain that comes from straightening out a locked joint.

Then the other leg slowly unfolds.

"Okay," he says through a pout. "I'll get the dumb shoes."

*   *   *

This is a story I wouldn't trade for anything. It was the day that Brian learned without a doubt that I meant what I said.

It had lasting effects in terms of numerous other trials. If I said we'd wait—for behavior to change, or for sit-in-the-chair-until-you-apologize-nicely time to pass—he knew I was prepared to wait forever; *I meant what I said.* And so we didn't have to; he obeyed. Almost all of the time.

Now, I could spend the rest of my days wondering if there might have been a better way to handle this. But then I would be fretting over spilled milk instead of noticing I needed to pour more. All I know is that I made measured choices, the best I was capable of at the time. Some days, simply hanging in there takes all you've got.

But that's not the point. The BIG lesson was this: it was the capacity to relax enough to allow visions of the ludicrous to dance in my head that turned a very questionable situation into a growing period for both of us.

There just is no point in hanging onto hostility, not when there's an outside possibility that humor and laughter can replace it and actually, perhaps, accomplish something. Sit back and really look at your situation. Almost anything that is extreme is bizarre. Almost any child is surprised by unexpected behavior, and ludicrous vision definitely warms the cold war or cools down the heated battle thereby altering behavior. And the best part is, it makes life easier.

There are numerous studies being done on laughter therapy. Many believe it heals not only mind and spirit, but body as well. The technique, whether it be old Three Stooges movies, cartoons or whatever, is even being used in some hospitals. "Laugh and be well," Matthew Green said. Clear back in 1737 he had this wisdom.

And what a fountain of humor children are. They are funny. Not always, but truly, they are funny. Try not to shut out your kids by hanging on to yesterday's troubles, whether they were initiated by the kids or not.

Learn to use humor—which can be a hotline to joy—as a transition tool. A transition not only from anger to laughter, but from anger to forgiveness, of ourselves and those around us.

"Be kind and compassionate to one another, forgiving each other, just as in Christ God forgave you" (Eph 4:32). So many times a good laugh lightens the mood and the spirit enough to let tenderheartedness seep in. Instant forgiveness can often follow before we even knew we had it in us.

"Of manners gentle, of affections mild; In wit, a man; simplicity, a child: With native humor temp'ring virtuous rage, Form'd to delight at once and last the age," wrote Alexander Pope. Let's hope a centuries-old message takes root in our hearts.

I have always been thankful that my parents both loved to laugh. It just came naturally to them, and so it did to me, and so it does to my sons. There is a warmth that surrounds laughter and permeates an entire house. Laughter fans an atmosphere of openness and helps us be comfortable with one another. It helps keep us from taking ourselves so seriously. It is an easy thing to share. It is catching.

When we can learn to laugh at ourselves, we have not only helped our own cause, but set a good example. We have taught our children that they, too, can—and *will*—make errors and still get through it all.

One day just a couple of years ago, Brian told George and me about a terrible day he'd just had. *Everything* had gotten fouled up. Each thing he did made the situation worse.

"You know how they say we learn from our mistakes? Well, I'm a bundle of knowledge today!" he said through a laugh.

Although the situation was confusing and caused him much anxiety at the time, he could laugh at himself now, and we could each laugh with him, and share some of our own embarrassing memories. We grow through those trying times. And we grow closer to one another by laughing together about them.

Yes, the shoe-store memory is a good one all right, and we've shared it many times. I think back to it now whenever I walk into a shoe store. I'm just thankful I didn't have to find out what it's like to sleep in one.

Dear Mom & Dad,
I lost my new glasses
in a six-foot-deep
mud hole. You'll be glad
to know I didn't dive in
to find them; I know
how you hate me tracking
up your clean floor.

· Seven ·

Haircut
Wars

Perspective

It *started with Bret when he was three years old, this thing about* hair. Up until then, it was just something that grew on his head. Oh sure, we'd had an occasional bout of entangled gooey gum wads, but other than that, hair was just something that basically took care of itself after a little washing and slicking down.

Then one day hair issues as we knew them changed.

Bret sat watching early Saturday morning cartoons—with the scissors. This was, obviously, an activity he had not checked in with Mom about. I walked around the corner just in time to see disaster strike. He had the scissors laid flat to his scalp on the very top of his head. The hinge rested just at the hairline of his forehead. The blades were open, as was his mouth. Before I could open mine, *CRUNCH!*

The scalping registered in my brain in slow motion. His trance-like state seemed to have nothing to do with the rest of his body. It was as though his arm and hand had acted on their own.

"Bret!" I screamed, but of course too late. I responded more to the horror of what had already happened than in warning. Two-inch, slick brown hairs slid down past his eyes and over his nose.

"Bret!" I repeated. "What have you done?"

"Nothing."

"Oh yes you have, you've cut a path down the top of your head!"

"No I didn't," he said, brushing the itchy telltale remnants out of his face.

"Go look in the mirror."

He strolled into the bathroom, pulled out the stool from under the sink and hopped up to mirror height. A look of terror captured his face and stayed there, thereby confirming my suspicions that his arm and hand had indeed acted on their own accord.

"My gosh, Bret, you're gonna have to get a crew cut to even that out. It's right smack down the middle!"

"I don't want to get a crew cut," he said, seeming surprised at the suggestion.

"Well, let's see what we can do then, if anything." I wet his hair and tried combing it this way and that. No matter what I did or how sopping I got it, it still wanted to flop apart at its manmade, one-inch-wide part. The fact Bret had slicker-than-slick, straight-as-a-board brown locks that always fell into bangs, no matter what, didn't help either.

"Well, I don't see much choice. Let's go into town and let the barber have a look to see if he has any suggestions." Bret wanted to try fixing it himself first. I handed over the comb. Then the brush. He finally gave up. Off to town we went.

The barber made the mistake of laughing when Bret walked in the door. I must admit, it was obvious why we were there, but Bret is a sensitive person. He was embarrassed, to say the least.

After setting him up in the chair, draping him with the striped cloth, turning him from side to side and whipping the remaining hair around a few times, the barber said there was only one alternative: crew cut. So be it. Closer to scalped was more the truth, but calling it a crew cut sounded better.

"It'll grow back soon," I said in consolation to a sick-looking little boy.

Well, Bret's hair doesn't grow very fast. It's the only time in his life he has ever worn a baseball cap with regularity, in contrast to his brother who seemed to have his head hermetically sealed by one clear through eighth grade.

Although this was a rather traumatic incident at the time, we all laugh about it now, just as the barber did the day Bret walked in to his shop. What a hilarious sight! But we weren't yet laughing. We had become temporarily blinded by the shock of it.

*　　*　　*

I think I'd be hard pressed to find a parent who doesn't have his or her own version of The Hair Horror Story. I even recall a couple neighbors of mine who didn't speak to each other for a while.

One daughter whacked the pony tail of the other's daughter right off at the rubber band. It had taken the victim's hair three years to grow long enough to make even that feeble pony tail. It was only five days later when it bit the dust. We're talking substantial tears at the time, although it's a warm-and-fuzzy chuckling experience when they get together and recount it now.

But hair has that wonderful way of giving one perspective: it will always grow back. No matter how terribly it's cut, colored or permed, you can always grow a fresh crop.

Yes. Perspective. A straightforward look at the reality of the situation. The notion that this, too—whatever it is—shall probably pass. It isn't usually, after all, life-threatening.

Consider all the options and outcomes. Is it something to find the funny side in, or something you should stop laughing about? Pondering the worst-case scenarios can often produce livable solutions. Bounce if off someone else. Stand back and take in the big picture. A runaway trip to Kmart does wonders for my perspective; so does a good hair story. And so Bret's hair finally did grow back. Nevertheless, I've always wondered if this, perhaps, was the incident that triggered Bret's haircut aversion. Let's just say it seemed as if from that point on he always wanted to wear his hair longer than we deemed appropriate.

"Can't I just let the back get a little longer?" he would always beg. Remember, this was in the same era as those white shoes kids wore; long hair was for hippies, not decent suburban cherubs.

Each time his hair would be hanging in his eyes or lapping over his collar, discussions about the next cut would begin. He was different from Brian, though; when the boom finally lowered, Bret would give in. Although the predicted grumbling got tiring, for several years it was still appropriate for me to tell the barber what Bret wanted.

I would stand where Bret couldn't see me because he couldn't turn his head because the barber had pushed his chin into his chest to cut the nape. Then I would hurl myself around in the background to get the attention of the barber and charade exactly what I was looking for. Bret always complained it was too short. I always said it was just right. Ah, the good old days.

Then he reached the age where showing up at the barber shop with him would have proved embarrassing for both of us. So before we would drop him off, George and I would give him lecture number 505 about how it wasn't worth the money to get only a smidgen cut off, and how he'd better come home looking as if he'd had a haircut.

Sometimes he did; sometimes he didn't. Lecture number 506 would follow about how money didn't grow on trees, then we would harrumph around a while until other things came along that just seemed more important to spend our energy on. Perspective.

We entered the next phase when Bret started driving and earning his own money from after-school, part-time jobs. What, he asked, if he paid for his own haircut? Shouldn't he have the right to get his hair cut any way he wanted if his own money paid for it? (Don't you just hate trick questions?) Also, by this time many were wearing somewhat longer hair at the nape of their necks, and so we said okay, within reason. We tried to be mature adults gaining perspective on the situation: styles had changed a little; passing math just seemed to be more important than the length of the hair on the back of his head. This doesn't mean there were never any grumblings, however.

"When I move out I'm going to grow hair three feet long," he would announce in an occasional huff.

"Fine. When you move out and are paying all your own bills, you can do whatever you want. You can sport hair down to your buttocks if you want. But not while you live in this house."

"I'm also going to drive you guys around in the back seat of my car," he would inform us, "with all the windows down and the stereo blasting." Seems hair started him on a roll that ended up encompassing all our trespasses, like requesting he not blow us to bits or start an earthquake with the volume. For Bret, his hair became symbolic of many things.

*　　*　　*

By the time Brian was old enough to whine about his hair, we had gained enough perspective to realize that hair just didn't matter that much in the grand scheme of things at our house. We were able to apply the "Ten years from now it won't . . ." guideline to issues of the hair. There were, I repeat, just too many more important things to save our energy for. Vital standing-our-ground concerns like curfew, alcohol, morality, grades and respect.

Besides, Brian's whining didn't come in the form of "I want to grow my hair longer." Noooo! When he was a freshman, Brian wanted a crew cut—and *flying lessons.*

To become a pilot had been this boy's goal since he could talk; a goal that never wavered then and still hasn't today. The notion scared me to death. All I could picture were airplanes spinning toward the earth to crash and burn. I could see my baby flying into an unpredicted hurricane. I could hear the newscaster reporting every detail of the tragic episode. But I am a parent. Conjuring up disaster comes naturally.

A friend of mine had a son who bought a motorcycle and she worried herself sick every time he pulled out of the driveway on it, imagining all sorts of grisly scenes.

Then one day she received a phone call. David, her nineteen-year-old man-child, had been critically wounded while water skiing, a sport he was well trained in. She'd better come to the hospital near the friend's cabin right away, the caller said. It was a several-hour trip.

David didn't survive. I cannot even imagine her grief. I could not understand how she could wake up in the morning with the knowledge her son was gone and even lift her head off the pillow. The Lord slowly nurtured her through the situation, but life will never be the same. She will never stop missing her son. And never in her wildest imaginations had she feared a freak boating accident. Her son had spent countless supervised hours as he was growing up learning the ins and outs of water safety. She feared the motorcycle.

I tell this incident because it harshly but instantly slams perspective into place. We cannot know, really, what tomorrow brings. We do not know, truly, what is in store for us and our children. No matter how much we worry, plan, maneuver, control and contrive, we cannot cover all the bases. We must not waste our valued time on this earth fretting over what doesn't matter. Perspective is imperative if we are to use our time with our children gainfully and joyfully.

Of course we will sometimes still worry, fret and mutter. We are human. We are parents. I am concerned every time Brian takes to the sky. But I realize he is fulfilling a heart's desire, something someone greater than I planted in his heart. I have considered that the drive to the airport is much more dangerous in terms of statistics than any flying time he does. (Perspective.) The day he came home with the tail of his shirt cut off—a traditional ceremony for first solo flights—was quite a celebration around this house. We were so proud, and he so fulfilled.

We cannot raise our children in a vacuum, sheltering them from the outside world. It is their right to explore enough to find out who they are and all they can be.

Please don't misinterpret what I'm saying. I am not promoting reckless living. I am simply trying to point out that perspective is easy to lose—in anger, in boredom, in fear, in narrow thinking, in lack of trust and wavering faith.

In a way, the entire purpose of this book is to help parents gain perspective. All of us as parents will experience lots of painful things, and many unforeseen blessings as well, as our children grow. A consistent effort to gain perspective—coupled with a mega-load of prayer, a sense of humor, and the freedom to allow for our own humanness—will help us to pass through the trying times, and to not miss the blessed ones.

"Finally, brothers, whatever is true, whatever is noble, whatever is right, whatever is pure, whatever is lovely, whatever is admirable—if anything is excellent or praiseworthy—think about such things" (Phil 4:8). What a balancer and reminder for our weary, worried minds. What a way to gain perspective. Who better to help us find it than God? I believe God grants perspective/wisdom through many avenues. For me, "Angel Vanessa" was one of them. And the year he sent her to me was a life-altering one.

*   *   *

Bret was nearing the end of seventh grade and had just received his latest in a long line of pep-up slips. For those not in the know, a pep-up slip is sent to parents to inform you that your daughter or son is either wasting his/her time, or missing assignments, or cutting classes, or failing tests and quizzes, or has a poor attitude, or . . . you get the picture. They are sent out so you can do whatever you can to help pep your child up, so to speak, in order that he or she will pull up to par.

Bret's offenses were in the wasting time, missing assignments, near-failing and general dinking around categories. He was, as I have mentioned before, a busy child. Not malicious or belligerent, simply busy. Certifiably, hyperactively busy.

At any rate, pep-up slip time used to send me into a tizzy. I was relating some of this to Vanessa, a woman who worked in the library at the junior high Bret attended. During both of my boys' reigns there I volunteered in the library once a week just to keep abreast of this creature called "junior higher." To be reminded that yes, kids that age are mean to each other. And yes, they all react to every little thing as a big deal. And yes, most parents are encountering many of your same woes. I learned this from the other volunteer moms.

So, like I said, I was shelving books while unloading my latest rankling to Vanessa. Now Vanessa knew Bret rather well because he also volunteered in the library several times a week during his homeroom class. He was what was referred to as an AV (audiovisual) person. If a classroom needed equipment from the library, Bret wheeled it to them and set up the projector. It not only helped the library, but helped him burn off a little energy as well. He reported directly to Vanessa.

When I was about halfway through my more-bad-grades diatribe—by no means the first she had listened to over a two-year period—the snow-white-haired Vanessa put down the book in her hands, turned to face me and grabbed me by the shoulders.

"Charlene, I have raised five children. My oldest child was a straight-A student and never gave me a lick of trouble. She is also one of the most miserable adults I know. Nothing is ever just right for her. She complains constantly. She is not a happy person.

"Bret, on the other hand, is one of the happiest people I've ever known. He is so willing to help and please. I honestly believe he's trying his hardest right now. It's just a difficult time for him.

"In the long run," she said, "what do you want for your children when they're grown? Don't you just want them to be content and happy? An impressive report card in their history isn't the key to happiness. Oh sure, it never hurts, but it isn't all that matters.

"Bret is a neat kid. I really like Bret and am always glad to see his smiling face come into the library. Lighten up, Charlene. Enjoy him. Grades aren't everything."

". . . whatever is true . . . whatever is lovely . . . whatever is admirable . . . if anything is excellent or praiseworthy . . . think about such things." Angel Vanessa bore the heavenly message in her own words. I knew God was speaking to me.

The light Angel Vanessa shed on our way helped us find perspective with our active little son. She had captured his strengths and made us look at them.

That same light kept us from breaking his loving spirit with our relentless monologues, badgering and disciplinary grounding over grades. It gently nurtured us into discovering the need Bret had for more acceptance and encouragement. Of course we continued to press for his best effort, but we had received a hearty lesson in unconditional love and balance.

We had been sorely missing many of his blessings because we were frankly too busy magnifying his shortcomings—a fruitless and shameful approach. Thank goodness the Lord wasn't missing a minute of Bret's or our needs and Angel Vanessa took the time to set us straight.

Bret's frequent, slightly-head-tilted smile and gleaming eyes seemed ever brighter from that day forward. And guess what? That happy, willing-to-please boy grew into a very responsible man. He still brings joy to those around him; he is dedicated to a good job; he is content and happy.

As a postscript to this selection from my memory portfolio, there was a time during that seventh-grade year when we felt forced to consider the possible "worst-case scenario" in an attempt to stand back and gain perspective. It just seemed good sense to do so.

What if he did flunk seventh grade? we wondered.

Then he would have to repeat it. Not life-threatening. Certainly not the worst thing that could happen to someone. We would survive. Angel Vanessa would have another year to warm his life by her delight in him.

But he did pass. Every grade thereafter. And he did move out and pay all his own bills. And he did grow his hair long; in fact he still has it. And that entire hair issue is still helping us keep things in perspective today. Even though it wouldn't be our choice in "dos" for his head, we love him no less because of it.

And as I sit and ponder his twinkly smile and his locks that are longer than mine, I become poignantly aware of perhaps an ultimate dose of perspective: his twenty-five-year-old, long, thinning crop and receding hairline make me realize that all too soon he's going to be bald.

·

Dear Anyone Who Will Listen,
I am Bret. The one
and only. I want a job,
an apartment, a roommate,
a motorcycle and
a dog. So what's all the fuss?

·

· *Eight* ·

The One
and Only

Individuality

After *my boys reached about fifth grade, I often found it necessary* to communicate with the little darlings via the written word—mostly my words to them. This was usually done in an attempt to accomplish a number of things, not the least of which was to keep the volume down.

If there was an important issue I felt had gotten lost or layered with the irrelevant, I found it a healthy exercise for me to talk about it on paper because there were no extra, heated words flying around. Only focus. Focus on the bottom line of the issue.

Sometimes spelling it all out helped me realize I had bought into a power struggle. If it was a subject or incident that seemed to escalate every time it resurfaced, bringing it up in a note at least gave me a chance to express my entire side of the matter without interruption. It kept both parties from retaliating with hasty, unwise words. It encouraged the balance of a loving, instructive, concerned delivery instead of a diatribe. Only the important got communicated on paper.

*　　*　　*

Such was the occasion on the day I wrote Bret an urgent note which demanded—I engaged my parental authority about as subtly as a two-by-four—that he write me a response. It was an unusual request, but what I needed that day couldn't seem to be accomplished via talking.

The letter was my attempt at getting inside Bret's head. I needed to find out what was really going on in there, and at the time, I was convinced he was trying to function on dead batteries.

It was June 1982, and Bret's junior-year report card had just arrived, confirming what we suspected. (It isn't true that life is one darn thing after another, it's the same darn thing over and over.) By the fuzzy hairs growing out of his chinny-chin-chin, he had managed to pass everything—but *barely* pass. He sure wasn't laying a good foundation for the rest of his life.

Let me point out that this was four years after Angel Vanessa taught me so much about perspective, about seeing the good side. Her lesson had slipped my mind for the moment.

A sense of urgency was sweeping me away: when was he going to trip his trigger and get with the program? Time was running out. I wrote a very brief cover note which pretty much expressed my "not-so-good foundation" worry.

Along with the cover letter I sent a mostly blank piece of paper that was to be filled out by Bret and returned to me. I wouldn't really say he was grounded, but I told him he could not exit his room until he made a sincere attempt to evaluate his own self by addressing the title I put on each side of that yellow ruled sheet.

The front side was labeled "Side I, Goals." At the top I wrote the following: "Dedicated to my mother whom I love and want to please today so she won't nag anymore." I thought that would elicit a chuckle and help us to pass through the front lines of this encounter. It did not; it coaxed out a groan.

The other side was labeled "Side II, Who I am, and what I have to do to achieve them (goals outlined on Side I)." All right, it wasn't very good grammar, but we both understood what it meant!

Bret disappeared behind his closed door to tackle the mission. I went on with daily household tasks, pretending I wasn't paying any attention to the ticking clock and my thumping headache. Within five minutes—oh, this ought to be good! I thought—he came bounding down the stairs two at a time (his usual pace) and delivered to me his responses.

As soon as I held the paper in my hands, Bret was out the front door with a brief comment as to his destination. After all, writing the note was all I had requested; waiting until I read it was never mentioned. And so as I heard the sounds of his car taking off down the street in the background, I approached "Side I." I did not need to pour a cup of tea to get me through these two pages; his entire outpouring was only two paragraphs long.

"My goals in life," he wrote on Side I, and I change not a letter, "are to get a job that I like, one that will suit my perticular needs, to get an apartment or rent a house (and then later on probably buy a house near a lake) with a roommate, preferably Paul, Joe, and/ or Tony. Buy a motorcycle and live in a warm climate. And then learn good penmanship. [His attempt at humor.] Also I want a *dog*!!!!!!" "Dog" was underlined five times.

It sounded to me like Bret was continuing that "happy" and "contented" course which Angel Vanessa had pointed out four years ago.

So far, his note wasn't bad. In fact, I was a little taken aback with his long-range plan. I don't know what I expected, but it wasn't something so . . . so . . . normal-sounding and succinct. Hard to argue with. I couldn't wait, however, to find out just how, exactly, he planned on accomplishing all this. I flipped to "Side II."

"I am Bret. The one and only. What I have to achieve them (the goals) is the willpower to achieve them. If I want something bad enough sooner or later I will get it unless it was never meant for me to have."

"The one and only." I sat dumbfounded staring at the phrase. My heart, which had previously been twisted in knots of anguish, suddenly swelled with thankfulness at a son who could recognize his "one-and-only-ness"—and could point it out to me.

It was written with such conviction! It came right out of him within five minutes. I may not have known who he was and what he was all about, but he certainly did. It was probably hard for him to imagine what all the fuss was for. I suspect he chalked it up as "Mom off the deep end—again."

To this day, I continue to keep that piece of paper in a notebook with other valued treasures.

*　　*　　*

Bret has pretty much mastered his list of goals, now, and some more besides. I'm proud of that. But what really pleases me is that he continues to be "the one and only." His hair and his freckled nose, his adventuresome spirit and his sense of humor belong to him and him alone. There has never been, nor will there ever be, another exactly like him. And I don't know if I could have had that point driven home the way it was without his words to me that announced this miracle.

The unique and separate being that God creates when he breathes life into each one of us is something to be valued, treasured and explored with awe. David acknowledges to God, in Psalm 139:13 (KJV), "Thou didst weave me in my mother's womb." Notice he speaks of weaving, not using a two-ton stamping press. The imagery there is so beautiful: it is one of time-consuming, careful, exacting planning and execution. Scrupulous examination of any handwoven fabric reveals the different intricacies in warp and woof, tension and design, spinning of the yarn and dye lot. Each piece the unique outcome of the creator's vision.

Simply looking at the disciples Jesus chose to walk with him gives us a good study in the necessity, if you will, of individuality. Each came to him in a different way, and not all started out with the goodness one might expect: there was doubting and denying and deceit. There was questioning and impatience and unbelief. But each was selected for his own distinct personality to be used as the Lord saw appropriate for his works. Each a different part of "the body" with its own particular function to perform.

The very behavior patterns that led to Bret's pep-up slips and borderline grades are the same ones that allow him to bravely tackle new challenges and far horizons. The tireless energy that kept him on the move as a youth allows him, as an adult, to carry on until tasks are complete, to pursue until answers are found.

We are called to give thanks in all things. Not an easy charge. But the very things that seem so negative sometimes when the children are small can be their biggest assets when correctly channeled.

*   *   *

Take Brian. I always said about him when he was little, "He's going to be either President of the United States or a roller derby king." His stubborn, strong-willed little self seemed to leave no room for anything in between. But those traits also kept him from being swayed by peer pressure as he grew older. His cautious nature is one of my biggest "Thank you God" prayers because of the flying vocation he is pursuing. It also helped him nail a successful high-school wrestling career.

He will do nothing before his or its time. Nothing.

I have a picture of our boys that my father took when the three of them were on a fishing trip in New Mexico once. It is an outward symbol to me of how different they are from one another and how unique each of them is. It was taken during a fishing break when the boys—well, when *Bret*—decided they would go cliff diving.

They are mid-air, on their way down, down, down. Bret's body is in the shape of an arrow: straight, toes pointed, arms out and at a forty-five-degree angle back from his shoulders. His chin is tilted slightly upward as if drinking in the sky he parts. His long hair sails behind him. He is facing this dive and challenge with all he has.

Brian is to his left and slightly upward of Bret in the photograph. His short cropped hair is standing on end. His body can't quite seem to make up its mind between diving and assuming the fetal position. He is facing the challenge with reluctance, after standing on the cliff for a very long time until *he* finally decides he would be sorry if he didn't try it.

Brian is not a coward; Bret is not daft. They are both relatively brave and face life pretty straight—each at their own pace. They are simply learning how to do the best they can with what they have, as am I, as are all of us.

120

Bret's "one and only" message helped me with more than understanding him: it gave me license to tolerate and value myself and everybody else a little better. After all, I am a one and only, too.

Recently a Mother's Day ad campaign played on that sentiment. The words were always printed beside beautiful things—things they hoped the reading public would purchase for their moms, of course. But the message was super: "Mom, my one and only."

As I watched my boys grow in their individual characteristics, so, I realized, had George and I grown as parents. In a way, we are like babies when we start out with these children. Everything is new.

But we experiment, and corral our mistakes, hopefully learning from them. We function pretty much within our individual personalities, give or take several million compromises. In order for us to function as a healthy family without constant rocks in the works, all our little personality glitches need to settle into a pattern that fits, just like a 1,000-piece puzzle. Eventually, you have one big family picture.

Not only do you have the picture, but you have the results of mingled and mixed notions, stronger and weaker genes, like and unlike attributes. Variety within which, we hope, our children can find and strike a chord of balance. Just as I ushered spontaneity and zest into our family unit, so George, thank the Lord, brought steadfastness, wise caution, predictable strength, frugality and earnest stick-to-it-iveness. Our mates and children help fill in our missing links through their unique gifts.

Pondering the concept of individuality as it fits into the grand scheme of things suggests to me some added benefits of learning to ride bareback.

*　　*　　*

When rider and horse are free to feel the structure and essence of each other without cumbersome tack in between, they begin to respond to the slightest of adjustments: a rein drapes across the left of a neck, the horse turns to the right; a knee pressures in with the lightest touch, the horse responds to what he has been gently taught that means. They can feel the very breath of each other.

As they run together, the horse has the incredible ability to sense the difference between a rider who loves and respects him and wants to elicit the best that he has to give, and the one who wants to bully him around and make him what he should not have to be— trying to transform a plow horse into a high stepper. Or a cutting horse into a jumper.

A good match of horse and rider meshes the two, creating one moving object that can negotiate smoothly through thicket and valley. They have learned each other's foibles and strengths and know how to adapt to them.

Each may have to depend on the other one day to arrive safely at their destination. Sometimes the horse must carry the load; sometimes the rider must lead the horse through a rough passage. Sometimes one's instinct about a future obstacle is more accurate than the other's, and yielding becomes the safest choice.

Before yielding can be done with a trusting spirit, however, they have had to build that relationship. Learn each one's areas of might and limitation. Learn to compensate for the gaps and be grateful for the differences that actually strengthen their united capability.

When a rider mounts bareback and travels for any distance, he can feel the sweat of the working horse. The horse, by the same token, instinctively assesses the rider and appreciates respect. Appreciates that the rider has taken the time to learn enough about him to trust him enough to go without a saddle, and sometimes even without a rider.

The most important thing for the rider to know is this. *Each horse has to be ridden somewhat differently.*

Some will test you every time until you prove your endurance. Others need a heel-tap in the ribs to get them going. The secret is finding out who needs what. Heaven forbid you should heel-tap the one that's already bursting to gallop at breakneck speed, especially if you're heading for a cliff!

One of the differences in my boys can best be illustrated by the old draw-the-imaginary-line scenario. Here's the line, we parents would point out. Could be the line of tolerance, curfew, patience. Didn't matter; we all needed to know exactly where the line was to eliminate misunderstandings.

Bret would tap dance up to the line twenty times a day. The widest part of the side of his foot would skim that line, constantly making us aware of his presence, eliciting endless bouts of confirmation that we noticed he was approaching. When he did step on it and the boom would be lowered, he would retreat. He basically respected authority, if he knew it was issued with genuine concern for his well-being. But everyone was constantly aware of the line.

Brian, on the other hand, could go for long periods of time without even looking at the line. We could be lulled into forgetting there was one. He would happily be in his own little world, obeying and generally being an okay kid. Then suddenly, without warning, he would march up and stand smack on the line, looking us directly in the eye while cocking his hip and pretty much daring us to do something about it.

Disciplining Bret took endless wads of patience. Disciplining Brian took occasional miracles and a lot of planning ahead. We didn't want to break their fragile spirits; we wanted them to learn to trust and obey, God and us.

Right from the minute they appeared in this world the differences in their gifts—and the trials they presented—became obvious. Bret almost never wanted to nap. He preferred just closing his eyes for a while, then revving up full-steam again. He never did crawl, but was running by the time he was nine months old—before he even had a tooth in his mischievous little grin. He ate almost anything and demanded a lot of attention. He could outlast anyone at the end of the day.

Brian, on the other hand, was (aside from his dig-in moments) an easy infant. So easy, in fact, that it worried me. After all, all I had to compare him with was the very busy Bret. Why, I wondered, would Brian sit in a playpen and actually play with things? Although the happy sounds and the sitting still gave me welcome resting periods, I wondered: is something wrong with him? After all, Bret had quickly learned how to lower the sides and escape.

I decided Brian was doing okay when he sprouted a surprise tooth at four months. Then he started showing some of his true colors when he began to selectively spit out green and strained foods.

Bret wandered off in a department store when he was about three and I decided I'd teach him a lesson by letting him realize he was lost. No such luck; I followed him around for several minutes while he explored every nook and cranny in the place and chatted with everyone in his path. Brian, remember, hated everything new, including shoes, baby sitters and foreign territory. Until he got to be about five and decided the world was his to conquer.

*   *   *

It is so much fun to see the boys together now. They stand peering at one another, shaking their heads. Then they grin and start teasing or wrestling.

"Man," Bret will say, "how did this ever happen to me? How did I ever end up with a brother who's a jock? And look at that hair!" He said that the first time he saw the flat-top which Brian sports in the summer.

Brian, on the other hand, delivers the same types of teasing when it comes to his brother the "biker," with his passion for motorcycles.

I have noticed that some of their different tendencies seem to have traded places over the years. Bret, especially when it comes to engines, can now tinker around for a long time without getting restless. He truly enjoys the tinkering. Brian, although he sticks with a project until it is done, wants to get it done much faster. Conquer it, you might say.

But for the most part, their individual characteristics have remained the same, simply growing stronger as the years pass. And I would not change a one, although they were not, and are sometimes still not, always easy to comprehend. But then again, I guess *this* one-and-only isn't either.

•

Dear Mom,
Love ya!
Bri.

•

• *Nine* •

Learning to Eat Crow

Humility

It was a tough parental decision: how do we handle our third-grade son's getting kicked off the school bus?

Disciplining wasn't the toughest part. There was also the little matter of the total embarrassment that came with the entire episode. Our son had been kicked off the bus for *spitting*. For spitting *out the bus window*. And the spittle—wouldn't you just know it— accidentally happened to land on a car.

Well, I don't need to tell you that this is something George and I weren't mentally prepared to deal with. And, there isn't a chapter on spitting in any of the parenting handbooks I've read. Personally, I would have never believed it was actually my son who had propelled the ill-fated gob, except for the small fact that he admitted to it—without batting an eye. In fact, there almost seemed to be a hint of pride in his voice. Pride in his bull's-eye delivery.

So much for a mother's "accidental" version of the story.

Thus leading to the point of this chapter. Never, and I mean never, say that your child would never . . . (fill in any awful, mischievous, malicious, destructive, dishonest thing you can think of here). I repeat, DON'T SAY IT! Especially out loud within earshot of anyone. Most of all, never, but never, allow yourself to believe it. Because as sure as you do, you will experience lesson number one in Learning to Eat Crow, a handbook that should 1) be written and 2) be mandatory reading for all parents.

The warning has already been recorded in the Psalms. Psalm 31:23, to be exact. "Love the Lord, all his saints! The Lord preserves the faithful, but the proud he pays back in full." No mincing of words there. If the divine Word of God promises it, you can bet your parental reputation that it's true. And who better to deliver the humbling blow than your children?

Be aware, if you are new to adolescent short-circuiting, that you do not have a clue, not even a particle of a hint, as to their capabilities and spur-of-the-moment possibilities.

Now I'm pretty sure—although I have just fallen into the dangerous dark hole of Parental Assumptions by even saying that—that Brian didn't lie awake the night before, scanning through the endless realm of possible disgusting behaviors he might exhibit the next day. I assume—possibly my next naive error—that it just seemed like the thing to do on the spur of the moment. There was this boring bus ride. There was this open window. There was this car. There was this spit.

Or else he was dared. Always a possibility, especially with boys.

At any rate, he did it. And he got busted. And a letter was sent home saying that he could not ride the bus for the rest of the week (two days), and that he would be allowed back on the bus the next week, assuming, of course, that his renegade spitting-raid days were over.

Well now. Do we make this third-grader walk to school about a mile and a half, crossing numerous unguarded, dangerous intersections? Do we make him hitchhike? Or, as usual, do the parents really become the burdened ones because they now have to accommodate the penalty?

You guessed it. And I lectured him once for every revolution those car tires made, not only on the way to school but on the way home as well. Home: the place where he spent a good deal of time doing extra chores.

In the meantime, this whole spitting subject took on a life of its own. "Dad spits all the time," Brian said defensively. "What's the big deal."

"That's because I have an accumulation of saliva that needs to be released," my husband countered with a near-medical tone in his voice.

"So did I," Brian said.

"Well, I think you could have swallowed it since you were on a bus," George responded, somewhat flustered and caught in his own web.

"Well, why don't you do that then, Dad? Why do you spit and make Mom disgusted?"

Silence.

Then, "Brian, I don't spit on cars."

"Dad, it accidentally landed on a car." He looks straight in his dad's eyes. A trace of dishonesty flickers across his face. He is not believed. He is told that if he ever gets in trouble again for spitting, he will walk to school, even if we have to walk with him.

(Another warning: Don't make threats you are not prepared to deliver.)

To further complicate the issue, I was reared by a father who spits. So when I fell in love with another wonderful man who also happened to have this nasty quirk, I was already somewhat numb to the rather repulsive behavior, although I did occasionally make snide comments about the barbaric and distasteful habit. But when my baby got in trouble for it, spitting in general just seemed to resurface with a new, more powerful yuckiness. The discussion still goes on today.

In fact, in retaliation and to prove a point, I decided that I would start spitting every time my husband or son did it, just to show them how disgusting and embarrassing it really is. Due to some genetic malfunction, however, I seem to have no built-in knack for delivering the goods where I am aiming, and little droplets tend to spew all over *me,* not the sidewalk or lawn. This produces nothing but hysterical laughter from my family and very peculiar glances from strangers.

At any rate, I use this spitting saga as an example of a humbling experience which was a learning one for all of us as well. Even though Brian exhibited no outward remorse at the time, the spitting barrage was never repeated. And the old adage that parents are always modeling to their children through their actions was definitely reinforced.

Although children seldom admit that consequences or rules or disciplinary actions have any effect on them, it's one of those things you thankfully learn about them in hindsight: yes, with enough repetition, things do soak in. And I'm sure (egads! parental assuming is near-impossible to avoid) that Brian was embarrassed when he was hauled into the principal's office upon arriving at school that ill-spittled day. He often used a "big-deal," chip-on-the-shoulder attitude to cover embarrassment.

George, of course, learned that children mimic our behaviors and then come back to haunt us with them. I, of course, learned that retaliation often boomerangs.

Okay. So purposefully spit out a bus window my son may have done. But shoplifting? Never! I could be sure of that.

Right.

*   *   *

It was almost dinner time when the call came. Seems Brian, now nine, and a friend were being detained by security at a local discount store within walking distance of our house. Caught redhanded. The heist attempt? A box of cigars and a lighter. ("I'm positive my boys will never smoke," I had been heard saying. "They are dead set against it.")

In the first flush of humiliation, I assumed that probably everyone I knew within a fifty-mile radius had witnessed my son being carted into the security office. I hoped he hadn't been dragged through the parking lot in handcuffs or anything. I hoped nineyear-olds were too young for this treatment. I thought about me and my reputation, not only as a parent, but as a respectable human being.

The instinct to preserve one's own reputation is quite a normal reaction, but it needs to be overcome. It is not what's of utmost importance.

"Do nothing out of selfish ambition or vain conceit," the Bible says (Phil 2:3). In fact, your own pride can be the booby trap that sinks everyone. The minute you're off on yourself and how your children have let you down and how they've disgraced your family name and how you have been affected, you have conveyed the message that *you* are what is important here, not them or their behavior.

That is not the attitude the Bible is urging us to learn. The same verse continues, "but in humility consider others better than yourselves."

And as for your kids, your prideful agitating may possibly have clammed them up, so no further explanation and no apology is likely. It has shut down the lines of communication and their willingness to listen and learn.

It has separated you from them, thereby yanking away their safety net. It has given you the opportunity to miss them when they fall.

Once I was able to move past my first selfish instinct, what flashed through my mind next was of much more importance and consequence, and I could concentrate on the relevant:

Thank goodness Brian had been caught! What if he had learned that shoplifting was easy? Getting busted, I realized, was actually an answer to a prayer I had shot up years before. It was something I learned from another mother. We hope our kids do get caught so they learn right from wrong and suffer natural consequences, she said, that can detour larger problems down the road. I'd almost forgotten that prayer.

Yes. I needed to move past myself and on to the bigger picture. The guard had asked for his father or me to come down and get him. I thought about it for a moment and said his father would be there, an outward sign of the seriousness of the offense. (Also, I wouldn't have to be seen frequenting the security office. Okay, so I wasn't totally past myself and on to the important. But I was working on it.)

Before I hung up, I told the guard that it might be at least a half-hour before someone would come. Even though we were only a two-minute drive away, I wanted Brian to have time to sit there and sweat. Think about this mess. Fantasize about the cell door closing behind him. Receive an up-close-and-personal dose of humility.

Of course this was a first offense and the police were not summoned. But the guard had scared them; that was The End of Brian's shoplifting days. He was visibly shaken when he arrived home with George. Not a speck of bravado in sight.

I highly recommend praying that children will get caught in their wrongdoings, although, of course, we hope they never do anything that warrants entrapment. But then, that's unrealistic dreaming. They all take their turns. Especially, it seems, those whose parents speak the loudest, or let their judgments on your children's behavior show in their eyes. Like some old neighbors of ours.

* * *

They moved in when our boys were around three and nine. They had no children at the time and immediately became good friends of our family.

But I could occasionally see it in their eyes as they watched the endless stream of incidents at our house. That look that said, "Our children are never going to. . . ." I kept myself from responding to this subtle wave of know-it-all. After all, only one who's been there recognizes it.

And so they had their first child. And she was, much to my chagrin, a near-perfect little baby. Never seemed to give them a lick of trouble. Could say the alphabet—forward and backward—way before her time. Puckered up and whimpered when quietly issued a "no." Then, did not repeat the offense, ever again. I seemed to be the one who needed to swallow the know-it-all attitude. Maybe something about our parenting skills was totally lacking if two people could produce someone as perfect as this little girl.

Then, along came their son. Same parents. Same guiding hands. Different composition entirely. A one-and-only to behold. We'll call him Direct Path To Crow-Eating for short. He came out of the chute causing trouble. I hinted that it couldn't have happened to nicer people. I secretly celebrated each wrong turn that kid made because it did, after all, make *our* family life seem more normal. Well, maybe celebrate is too strong a word. I understood their trauma, and we became all the closer for it. We were bonded by "normalcy."

Their first child's behavior, it was decided, was a fluke. Pure grace. Yet she gave them cause to brave a third child who, as it turned out, was more like the second, thus proving our theory: Normalcy Consists of Trauma.

In the meantime, our boys continued on their "normal" path as well. One humbling episode brewed over a several-year period, and we knew nothing about it. Nothing.

* * *

Seems Bret did a lot of early-morning eating. After breakfast at home, he would go out for a bike ride to burn off some of that steam before the confinement of a classroom. What we didn't know was that he was stopping in at the Nelsons' and eating again. We're talking 7:30 a.m. arrival here.

All those mornings, the Nelsons were under the assumption that poor Bret was never served food at his house in the morning. Of course the truth was that he garfed down great bowls of it, then immediately burned it off. He was somewhat of a bottomless pit back then, and a skinny little twig as well. And so the Nelsons would kindly give the big-eyed, drooling Bret a portion of whatever was on their table, almost every single morning of his life during that time. And here we were building a questionable reputation all the while. No visible signs of attack; just a silent assault on our parenting prowess. Also, over this time period, Bret was building a solid and mutually caring relationship with the Nelsons. Not only with two of their boys with whom Bret spent a lot of time, but with their parents as well. Four more ears to hear about his trials and tribulations. Four more eyes to greet him with a friendly look of love. Two more mouths to reinforce parental perspective.

They have been, and continue to be, a second family to Bret. I will be eternally grateful that God sent the Nelsons into his life.

Webster's New World Dictionary refers to humility as "absence of pride." That is surely something parents need to get a handle on when one of their children finds another source of guidance, solace and love. It is easy for jealousy to rear its head and strip the goodness out of something. Thankfully, only mild bouts of that occasionally swept over me when it came to the Nelsons, and they were kept in check. Somehow, as with Angel Vanessa, I managed to see their genuine affection for Bret as another of God's vessels. God's hands. Hands to guide and love and care. Indeed a humbling vision.

Sometimes more patient hands than mine. Often an easier ear to talk to than a parent's. Thankfully, we all had the same moral standards and ideas about discipline because the Nelsons certainly had an influence on him. Thankfully, Bret felt free to reach out to them when we were not available, and they, in turn, felt free to let us know of their concern for and enjoyment of our son.

They helped Bret and us through several bouts of unrest. The Nelsons were there to catch the overflow. To help Bret land on his feet. To serve as liaison.

And eventually, years down the road, we all sat and laughed at the reputation we had built at their house for sending our child out in the morning hungry. A small price to pay for encompassing love.

*   *   *

Yes, there are countless humbling experiences in our memory portfolio, but not all of them come from negative and misunderstood behavior. The most enlightening and awesomely humbling times happen when, like the power in the wand of the fairy that transformed Cinderella, God touches us, *touches us*—through our children.

As the Nelsons' hands served as hands of God to guide, nurture, teach and help Bret grow in love, so I see our children as God's same instruments for us. They are his children he has entrusted to us, yet they also serve as his vessels. These revered, humbling, grace-filled experiences our children bring to us can be delivered through the smallest of hands or the briefest of moments.

They come to us like beautiful gifts from the sea; natural pearls. Should we be there to accept them, we can string them together, affording us the most beautiful strands of memories.

*   *   *

One day several years ago I was in town running errands. Boring, tiresome tasks that left me rather weary. When I returned to my car, which was parked on a side street, I found a ripped piece of brown paper stuck under my windshield wiper. On it was scrawled a penciled note:

"Hi Mom! Love ya, Bri."

I unlocked my car and sat in the front seat clutching that piece of paper, staring at it, smiling, tearing up a bit, smiling some more. Reading it over and over. My harried day had been transformed into a moment of warm fuzzy. How blessed was I to raise a son who would take the time to touch me in that way. How wonderful was my God to perk up my tired spirit.

Of course Brian had no idea exactly how profoundly he had touched me. He had simply gone to his car on his sophomore-year lunch break, run across his mother's car on the way either to or from his venture, and decided to leave her a little note. No big deal to him. But it certainly was to me.

I not only felt the love of my son, but the love of God as well. That note hung on my refrigerator for years, perking me up every time I looked at it. It was a reminder of all the times the boys were messengers and examples of love. Students and teachers alike.

Daily our children challenge us, giving us reason to continue growing and learning; giving us cause to draw nearer to God.

George and I both spent self-indulged hours watching Brian coo and smile up at us with total trust in his eyes. What a model he served as; an example of a refreshing way for us to approach our Father, rather than always with an endless list of "Help-me-Lord" prayers.

There were so many times I needed to apologize to Bret for my impatience. "That's okay, Mommy" always followed directly and freely on the heels of my apology, modeling Christ's instant forgiveness upon repentance. Children seem to instinctively know that it is best to forgive and let go.

Both of the boys presented us with cratefuls of scribbled drawings, many totally undecipherable as to intent. But of course we treasured the sincerity of the spirit with which they were given to us. Did we realize that God was teaching us and our children about his appreciation of our heart-given attempts, no matter how feeble the results may seem?

Recently I spoke with the mother of a seven-month-old child. She was relating the stories of how many parents spend so much time complaining. "It tends to be a habit, complaining about your kids," she said. "One mother complained about all the dirty diapers, and how sore her breasts were from nursing. . . ."

"Mine is a unique situation," she said. She and her husband had spent four years trying to conceive their son Hank: infertility treatments, stress, doubt, faith. "We waited so long to have him. It was a miracle that we were finally able to conceive. Well, I cherished every dirty diaper because it meant everything about him was working properly. My breasts were sore and it was good because it meant he could suck really hard and get nourishment."

She went on to talk about some mothers who complain about getting up at night. Her experience was viewed through different eyes.

"I enjoyed Hank at night," she said, "because it was such a quiet time. He would fall asleep at my breast and I didn't put him down right away. I would inspect his fingers and toes and see how he was growing. I thank God every day. I thought after a while the shininess of this brand new miracle would wear off. But it doesn't. I get him out of the bathtub and he will be all squeaky clean and I am thrilled all over again."

Thrilled and humbled by God's goodness, this precious gift we call our child.

*   *   *

Children humble us through their unthinkably bad choices, through their precious examples, through their mere existence. But there's yet another way, and perhaps I can best show you through the following story rather than try to explain it. I think you'll get the drift. I know I sure did.

One day about five years ago Brian and I were chatting. Suddenly he responded with something that was mean and cutting. Cutting to the quick.

I stood speechless for a moment, flushed with heat. My eyes stung with tears, my throat was tight. I finally squeaked out, "Brian, that was so mean and wounding. I can't believe you said that to me."

"Mom, I hear you talking to Dad like that lately."

He used an unrelenting tone that was far from his usual friendly and warm approach to conversations.

Part of me wanted to crack him across the face. The other part, the spiritual part, stood convicted on the spot. Brian spoke Truth.

*   *   *

I have now come complete cycle on the topic of humility: George was busted for his own spitting; I was busted for my own sharp tongue. We each received a holy pie in the face, lessons sent by the Lord and delivered by no less than the hands of our children.

And in between those cultured, manmade pearls on our strands of memories we are blessed to be able to string the finest pearls of natural beauty, God's humbling gifts to parents—theirs simply for the taking.

•

**Dear Dad,
I know Mom's
in there somewhere;
I saw her eyes blink.**

•

· *Ten* ·

Mommyland

Survival

Now hear this, all mommies! Even though I am spending the entirety of these pages imploring you to not miss your kids, I'm here to tell you that high on the list of things you can do to insure that is to depart from them as often as necessary, even if it's only for a mind's ride to Mommyland.

If you've never heard of Mommyland, I'd volunteer to take you by the hand and lead you there right now, but each mommy has to find her own place. Her own little haven. Her own exciting or brain-dead journey—whichever is in order at the moment to help her hang on to sanity.

"When I go there," my good friend Mary Beth ("Oh child of God") said, "I am not necessarily dreaming of butterflies and soft things. Sometimes I am trying to figure out a problem and you can't do that when people are bothering you all the time, so you just sort of go there and do some problem solving or whatever needs to be done. Sometimes you just go there to concentrate on cleaning the bathroom floor without interruptions."

So there you have a little glimpse into a corner of Mary Beth's Mommyland. And she, for the record, is the one who coined that phrase. Put title to the trip. Nailed down the journey-via-osmosis.

Now in my own Mommyland, I would not allow the thought of a dirty bathroom floor. I would consider it nothing short of a violation of my personal Mommyland principles. Oh sure, I may lock myself in the bathroom to try to find Alice's hole that leads to Mommyland, but I would not push a mop while I was doing it.

For me the truth is, the bathroom has never been conducive to Mommyland, even though I've experienced numerous aborted tries at capturing it there. Incidents like the following.

*　　*　　*

I poured an ice-cold glass of water in preparation for my ascent. "Hold my calls and don't knock on the door," I said as I disappeared up the stairs toward the haven of The Bath, leaving my family standing speechless in the kitchen.

It had been one of those days, leading to THAT moment that triggered my plight. I absolutely needed to be where the rest of them were not. My instinctual fight-or-flee mechanism had kicked in, then gone "tilt!" Options closed. Fleeing was the only choice.

Upon entering my oasis—my envisioned route to Mommyland— I firmly closed and locked the door behind me, then leaned against it for a moment just in case anyone should be following me.

Pause. Listen. Exhale. Proceed.

I adjusted the flow of water to the perfect fog of steam and stared into the mist for a moment. Then I poured a stream of bath beads tubward to silken the water. Essence of magnolia wafted up my nose. It was delicious.

The small glow of light from a match illumined my face as I swept around the room lighting the candles I unearthed from the closet.

Like a snake's skin, my clothes were shed. I placed the sweating glass of water on the tub's edge and set my new novel within arm's reach.

As my body cut through the bubbles, I knew everything was in order; life was as it should be. I slipped my lip over the edge of the refreshing cool water and took a sip. Aaah. For two minutes, I just soaked and stared at the flickering flames of candlelight. Mommyland was just around the corner.

After that brief, life-altering pause, I was finally ready to enter. I opened the book to page one.

Being a short person, I found that by the time my feet touched the end of the tub, my head was practically submerged under the glorious bubbles. I scooted, slid and rearranged for quite a little while before grabbing one more sip. I would have to sit up if I was to read. And so I did.

About the time I got to the third paragraph, my forehead had broken out with little beads of perspiration, and my nose, too, and my glasses began fogging up and slipping off my face. When I reached to shove them up, the side of my book accidentally found its way into my tranquil water.

I tossed the soggy mass overboard. I just soaked and stared at the mesmerizing flames. Mommyland popped back into view.

My back started getting a kink. I decided since I didn't have to read anymore, I could slip back down into the tub. As long as my nose was above water, I'd be okay. Having my eyes at water level soon led me to the discovery that my bubbles had disappeared, and a sort of a milky oil slick floated in its place. I closed my eyelids and took a deep breath. I was beginning to feel ill.

Of course I was beginning to feel ill! I never *have* handled heat very well.

I bolted up in the tub as though I had been electrocuted. Deja vu. Why can't I remember hot baths aren't for me? They are not the yellow brick road to Mommyland, they are a slide straight to insanity.

In one motion I pulled the plug and turned on the shower to rinse the scum off my body. As I stood in a foot of draining water with the shower beating on my head, I tried to think this through.

Didn't Doris Day always take a bubble bath to calm her down? Don't French women do this as the epitome of luxury and relaxation? Haven't I read this scenario in countless romance novels?

Is something wrong with my hormones?

I brusquely finished showering and soon appeared downstairs with my empty glass.

"I thought you were going to take a long bubble bath," my husband said.

"Well," I snapped, "you thought wrong!"

*　*　*

Even though baths may be the Mommyland doorway for many, they are certainly not mine. Flickering flames, however, are. And, lucky for me, I can light a candle on my kitchen table right in the midst of chaos. All I need do is stare at it.

But what if the kids are hanging on your legs and you can't isolate yourself?

Find your own express lane to Mommyland and hop on it. Even

as the child screams and bellows, you can learn, through condition-
ing, to depart into the silent corner of your Mommyland. Physically, your leg may be functioning as a hanger for infant bodies, but
mentally, you are gone. Zap. Disappeared. Safe. Sheltered.

Mary Beth recently took an automobile trip with her brother—
and five children. The kids were carrying on as kids do in a car and
Mary Beth skipped out to Mommyland, even while she was driving.
Even while the volume rose.

Her brother drew her back into his world, however, whining
about the noise. "Don't get involved with the kids," she told him.
"Stay out of it. Stare into space. Think about other things and
pretty soon you won't hear the noise. What you need to do is focus
away from the kids."

Mary Beth claims Mommyland is self-preservation. An escape.
"You escape to protect yourself." And sometimes you can't get
there by yourself. That is when Mommyland tools come in handy.
Tools like a flickering flame, or a tub, or a book, or a lawn mower.

Lawn mower? Yes. Mary Beth also finds Mommyland behind the
loud—and that is the key element here—mower. The noise, she
claims, blocks out all other distractions and allows her to concentrate. Personally, I find mowing in Mommyland about as appealing
as mopping floors, but it works for her, and that's what counts.

Mary Beth also believes that husbands are the biggest infiltrators
of Mommyland when they are around.

"I will be concentrating on a book or a problem or whatever and
the kids are screaming 'Mommy! Mommy! Mommy!' trying to get
my attention. But I'm successfully blocking them out. Then my
husband will call my name and say, 'Mary Beth, they are trying to
talk to you.' "

And so she responds to the children and then "disappears" again.

She says her mistake has been in not telling Dave she is "gone," so that he doesn't accidentally call her back.

Mary Beth started honing her technique when she was in college. She had to learn to study through dorm noise and constant interruptions. She started referring to this "place" she went to as Mommyland when she became more aware of the need for it—immediately after she became a mother, of course.

She holds the conviction, and I agree with her, that if you can't learn to find Mommyland, you have possibly left the door open for child abuse. So Mommyland is protection for your family as well.

"There is a part of me," she admits, "that feels guilty about all this Mommyland and escaping thing." Mothers are good at mustering up guilt, aren't they? Especially toward themselves. But, "I feel like there is energy being drained that I don't have at that point," she continues. And after she analyzes it for a moment, she knows it is not self-indulgent, but merely protective.

And you have to be able to go there without baggage. "A place to work things out and let things go," she says. I ditto that reasoning. If you take all the mess with you, you might as well not have left.

Lest you get a wrong picture of my friend, she deals out more hugs and has more patience than anyone I know with three children under age seven. Perhaps Mommyland is why. It is a place to be good to yourself, therefore letting you refuel so as to pass on the goodness to others.

She comes from a long line of Mommylanders. She says her mother and her grandmother used to go there, and one of her daughters already does.

Mommyland, she clarifies, is not to be confused with The Silent Treatment. The Silent Treatment, which can cause undue stress for our children, comes out of anger and shows on your face. Mommyland is motivated by a different need and appears as zoning out.

And not to worry about your children getting in trouble and going unnoticed while you've departed. "There are certain sounds your kids make that let you know they are in trouble." And we all know exactly what she's talking about. They're the ones that make you hang up the phone or run outside. They are different than argumentative, tantrum, tired or whining sounds. They possess their own built-in express lane to Mommyland.

For Mary Beth, Mommyland is a totally isolated place. "I never want anyone there. I come out of Mommyland to discuss things," she says.

As for me, Mary Beth is part of my Mommyland. As is Mary, my Keeper-of-the-Big-Wheel-Brigade partner. There are conversations we have had and continue to have that connect us and our Mommylands. Things we know about each other that need no explanation. Experiences and thoughts we have shared that need only be referred to, and we are immediately washed with oneness. My Mommyland has a need for these kinds of connections.

As of this writing, in nine days I will be flying to Oregon to visit Mary. This is a vacation we have talked about for many years. It is one I sorely need. It is one we will take together as we leave her house for a few days to stay ocean-side and ponder. Share. Sit together in silence. Perhaps enter my version of the epitome of Mommyland: an altered state in an altered state.

She has, in the last six weeks or so, sent me a series of postcards, one more beautiful than the other. The last is a picture of a giant blue-green wave crashing and exploding high into the air. It is full of movement, white foaming release. Power. Tranquility. It beckons. She knows this about me.

"Yes," She wrote on the card. "Can you hear the sound of the ocean? Come west to renew the spirit and your creative center. Can't wait to see you and share good times. Love, Mary."

I wept when I received this card. Its timing, as usual, was exact. I celebrated and praised God for sending a friend into my life who makes a connection with me that goes beyond words. My personal Mommyland would have a missing link if there weren't people in my life I could share portions of it with.

* * *

Now my husband and I definitely share a lot of things, but Mommyland isn't one of them. I'm sure he has his own counterpart to this place in space, but it cannot truly be Mommyland. He is barred by virtue of testosterone.

Whether your own personal Mommyland takes in others or not, I do believe that finding others who truly understand your parenting plight is imperative. Like that all-day seminar George and I attended. Just seeing all the other bleary-eyed parents wandering around looking for answers gave us heart. "I am not alone" is always a comforting discovery.

The Chicago Tribune Magazine recently ran a lengthy article entitled "No mom is an island." It covered the plight of stay-at-homes who have no one else in their neighborhood to talk to and no other children for their children to play with; and it looked at the plight of working moms trying to find those get-together times for themselves and their children.

"Mothers need to find those colleagues with whom they can swap ideas and on whom they can lean for support. As a consequence, they have been inventing new ways to re-create the coffee klatches of the past, to create family-support and parenting-education groups," wrote Florence Hamlish Levinsohn.

The article listed many formal groups that meet. People reaching out to connect any way they can. There was even a 1988 "Directory of Self-Help and Mutual Aid Groups" talked about which listed "more than 60 parent groups in the Chicago metropolitan area, including three father's groups, 26 single-parent groups and nine groups for parents under stress."

Whatever you need, reach out and find it. Don't let your endeavors as a parent become isolated ones. We need more than children in our lives; we need each other. Problems we deal with on our own are usually magnified. Answers are often found lingering over a cup of coffee.

Although some of these groups lean more toward the educational end, I personally think the informal gatherings can be more relaxing. They are not "one more thing I have to be learning." They are a place, like Mommyland, to just hang out. Tell the truth. Listen. Laugh. Look forward to.

The article covered Family Focus centers. They offer classes in child-rearing, "but their major thrust is to provide a comfortable place for mothers with children under 4 years to spend a morning chatting with other mothers while their children play in another room attended by caregivers."

I think how lucky Mary and I were, as well as many other mothers and children in our neighborhood, to simply be able to walk across the street and not pay any dues for this much-needed camaraderie. There was always someone in need of a break. We could wander from door to door saying, "Is it break time yet?" One could always find a taker. Sometimes we would sit and chat together while the kids played in the yard. Sometimes we would unburden each other from our tykes for a spell, knowing our turn would come, too, for some time off.

*   *   *

Here are a couple of things mothers had to say about their involvement with the Family Focus centers that, in their own way, paralleled my neighborhood experience.

Karen Ami MacRoberts, sculptor: "I didn't start coming until he [2-year-old son] was 18 months old. I wish I had started coming sooner. I'd probably be a little more sane now."

Jan Sokolow, designer of computer systems: "I learned to relax about teaching him [son] all kinds of things he wasn't really ready for. You've got to let them develop naturally."

Stories about other groups covered in that article pretty much proved the same point: no mom is an island. Right.

*   *   *

But sometimes we need to be *on* one. Sometimes other mothers aren't around. Sometimes we don't want them, either. Sometimes what we really need is to recharge our spiritual batteries.

Even Christ went off alone to pray. So, too, we need to be alone and focus on God, our unending source of renewal. Let God remind us that what we are doing has value and eternal results. Recapture perspective. Lay down our burdens before him.

Jesus broke away from the pressures to rest and to regain perspective. And he made time to pray, even when it wasn't very convenient or comfortable. Sometimes, that's what we've got to do. Hire a sitter, just once, and spend a morning walking in your local park. Take a Bible and notebook; sit and read. Make notes to yourself. See if it isn't worth the sitter fee.

Taking one weekend a year to go on your church's weekend

retreat for women or couples, or to attend a marriage seminar, may be the best thing you can do—*for your kids*. Yes, it'll take a lot of planning and juggling. But the richer you are as a person, the more you have to offer as a parent.

*   *   *

Other times you simply need to enter the glorious privacy of Mommyland. Often nothing more than a sixty-second burst of self-indulgence, because that's all there's time for.

For example, not only do I like flickering flames, but I find certain fragrances have a calming effect on me. Another cheap "tool" of the Mommyland trade at my house is incense. Strawberry or patchouli, to be exact. I watch the flickering flame of the match lighting the compressed, soon-to-multiply fragrance. Aaah. Something to camouflage the odor of the stopped-up garbage disposal. Something to remind me that all can become more than it seems. Like watching green vines sprout Heavenly Blue Morning Glories. Or a cricket chirping a pulsating beat. Or the call of a red-winged blackbird that reminds me of the sounds I used to listen to as I sat by the creek as a youth.

Look for joy in simple pleasures. You'd be amazed what a mini-retreat that can be. Watching the birds splatter around in the birdbath. Deciding to use the kids' nap time to lie in the grass or see if you can still climb a tree or dig out an old favorite album.

Give yourself a pedicure. Put a cool washcloth over your eyes. Make yourself a bowl of popcorn. Dig out old pictures. Keep some bubble stuff on hand and blow bubbles out your back door. Fantasize about being in the mountains, inhaling the fragrance of burning logs and watching eagles soar.

Clear your brain. Be still. Refresh. Explore Mommyland, whether it be for one minute or the miracle vacation like mine that lasts a week. Dust, dirty dishes, unmade beds will still be there when you return, and perhaps they won't seem as burdensome after a pause for your cause. And guess what? The same goes for your kids.

I would suggest practicing skipping in and out of Mommyland when things are calm. When you feel put together and unhassled. Get familiar with all the paths that may lead you there; don't get discouraged by the ones that don't. There are endless possibilities.

Be aware, however. There are some occasions when Mommyland just doesn't cut it. It isn't the miracle cure for everything. I wouldn't be honest if I led you to believe that.

*   *   *

Mary Beth's middle child, now five years of age, was diagnosed with cancer over two years ago. She and her husband have been holding the family together while their second-born, Laura Jane, undergoes chemotherapy. She has been in remission for some time and treatment should be drawing to an end soon.

Endless trips to the hospital in the city. Sickness. Fear. Anxiety. Blood transfusions. Trying to come up with last-minute babysitters during crisis. Making it through the days without sleep during the nights. Drug deliveries from UPS. Learning about central lines and what to do in case of emergency. And so on and so on and so on. They had just finished a nine-day stay in the hospital, one of their scarier stints. Finally, they were home and life could return to what had become their normal. Then, Laura Jane took a bicycle spill and broke both bones in her left forearm—the arm to which the thumb she sucks is attached. I received this news the afternoon it happened.

Ring, went my phone.

"Hello," I answered.

"Sometimes," Mary Beth said, "Mommyland just isn't far enough away."

•

Dear George,

I am thankful we hung

together and observed one

another while the

boys were growing up. Now,

in our sweet aloneness,

we can reminisce not only

about them, but about

the US they helped to evolve.

•

· *Eleven* ·

After They're Gone

Empty Nest

I just hung up the phone from a lengthy conversation. I've been chatting long distance with my dad. Notice I didn't call him the man who used to be my dad. Nor, now that I'm a grown woman with grown children of my own, do I refer to him as Victor. He has always been, is now, and will continue to be Dad to me.

Up until the time my mother died fifteen years ago, I called her Mom. Not Nellie. Mom. I cannot imagine thinking of her in any other terms. She defined the role of mother for me, and thankfully it was a happy and fulfilling one.

Not that she didn't also become a friend as I grew older—someone to laugh with, cry with, share with. But the "friend" part of our relationship could not be separated from the mother/daughter bond, nor would I have ever wanted it to be.

We never stop being Mom and Dad. Although our parenting roles, attitudes, responsibilities and viewpoints may fluctuate, diminish, rekindle and settle over time, our kids are still our children and we are still their parents.

Amy Grant, a major presence in Christian music, recently did an interview for *Today's Christian Woman* magazine. Throughout much of her discussion with author Dale Hanson Bourke, she spoke of how different life is now that she's a mother.

During one point in the interview she made the following observation: "I don't think kids can ever know their parents like other people can know them. But once you have kids of your own, your perspective on your parents changes."

By the same token, becoming a parent adds another element to who we are and influences how others see us.

"Amy is still the charming, husky-voiced star who burst onto the contemporary Christian music scene as a teen," Bourke wrote. "But being a mom defines Amy in ways that make her more beautiful and vulnerable than she's ever seemed before."

I know for a fact that bearing a child did not automatically make me physically more beautiful: stretch marks, hair that sometimes didn't have time to be washed, stress lines that attacked my face during the wee hours, then etched a permanent map around my eyes . . . but I know what Bourke spoke of. It is a flowering. An opening of things in us we didn't know were even lying dormant: a new softness, a deeper love, the literal flowing of milk through our bodies.

* * *

Becoming a parent has something of the same effect on fathers. I watched my six-foot-two, two-hundred-twenty-pound, size-thirteen-ring husband—whose moves have never been mistaken for a ballerina's—become transformed at the dressing table the day we brought Brian home.

Brian was born during a time when fathers were not allowed to touch their babies until they were out of the hospital. The fathers had to be in the car, for that matter, because the nurse carried the babies alongside the wheelchair and handed them over to the mother after she was safely planted in the front seat.

George chose to wait until we arrived home to try his first hands-on experience. In fact, he changed Brian's first home-soiled diaper. I stood by his side and talked him through the task. Tears welled in my eyes and an unknown corner of my heart lit up as I watched this massive man and his massive hands exhibit the feather-light, gentle and careful touch of a brain surgeon.

Okay, so the diapering job itself wasn't so hot; but the kind of love and awe that poured forth from the imposing form of my husband into the tiny baby that lay totally vulnerable at his finger-tips . . . that picture, that transformation, that first bonding gesture, instantly revealed a part of George that neither of us knew was buried inside, waiting to burst forth with this magical encounter.

And this opening, this flowering, this unveiling of more than we had been, instantly became a new and beautiful part of *us*. A part of the *us* that was created and revealed after the birth of Brian. A part of the *us* that is left now that the children are gone.

And since *us*, for the most part, is all that there is now, I am acutely aware of the importance of having hung together while the children were home. Observing one another. Catching action glimpses of each other in settings that will never be repeated. Learning to share the new-found burdens. Delighting in the surprises of hidden talents. Helping each other let go.

*   *   *

So here we are now. Alone.

But not really, because there's a spoiled-rotten dog and a bird to keep us entertained. And, thank goodness, they actually do. (There used to be a gerbil but . . . may he rest in peace.)

Why, just this last month we've taken Butch, our black-and-white-looks-just-like-a-border collie-but-is-really-a-mutt dog, to the vet three times. Each time for the same condition: fleas and his allergic reaction to their bites. He also keeps us busy screaming "STAY OFF THE NEW COUCH!"

Then, of course, there are all those trips we take outside with him because he seems to have a bladder the size of a pea and a thirst that causes him a daily water intake the size of Lake Michigan. And we don't have a fenced yard. And he runs away if he's not on a leash. And so we are kept very entertained running in and out the door with him. And then giving him treats for his "good boy" duty because . . . because . . . I don't know why we ever started rewarding him for going to the bathroom. But after six years he's grown to expect one and he follows us around barking if we forget.

As for Nellie, our blue/green parakeet—whom we named after my mother, and who we didn't find out was a male until after we named him Nellie—we must spend countless hours repeating the same phrases over and over and over so he can learn to say them back to us when we walk into a room. Things like "Hello" and "Pretty girl." He's also finally mastered an incredible wolf whistle. Yea, Nellie!

Getting back to the new couch for a moment, here's something I'd like to warn you about: By the time you send your children to college or off to the military or whatever, everything in your house is in shreds and *you just can't stand it anymore.* "Our baby is twenty years old," you say to your spouse one day. "Why does it look like preschoolers still live here?"

Not only that, but you have entered your own personal mid-life crisis, thereby compounding everything but the interest on your money—which you haven't saved anyway, so not to worry.

Lest you should start thinking conditions around our house are bleak, that's not true. Although nothing above is untrue, what I haven't mentioned yet is the up-side of the empty nest: we can now have our meat loaf with onions in it again without watching someone pick them out or tell us how disgusting they are. We can also run around the house naked. Although we don't very often because of the dog.

We spend a lot of time trucking to Kmart together. (See, I don't always go it alone.) I don't actually know why we go there so often. After all, we need less toothpaste, less soap, less shampoo. . . . Maybe it's because we have more time to read the sale flyers now, thereby becoming aware of things we didn't know we needed.

Something we found ourselves doing the first year Brian was gone, and I'm sure we'll repeat this year, is watching other people's kids wrestle and listening to other parents' children sing. After spending so many years acquiring such well-seasoned bleacher buns, it seems a shame to let them go to waste.

In terms of that extra living space empty nesters dream about, we're not quite as far ahead of the game as planned. Although the tiny bedroom is now my office, Brian still comes home several times during the year and spends summers here, so his room isn't freed up yet. And heaven forbid we should alter anything.

On the storage front, we've gained no ground, although that's not all bad. We've kept the wind-up swing, the playpen, the Tonka trucks, Fisher Price toys and highchair for so long now "just in case," that we have decided we might as well hang on to them for our grandchildren.

Okay, so the basement and the attic will never be cleared out like we thought they would "when the kids leave," but somehow we believe that watching another generation wind, push and cart their parents' things around will bring more satisfaction to us than a few empty spaces.

*   *   *

On a more serious note, just as my parents will always be Mom and Dad to me, so George and I will be to our boys.

Bret recently visited for a week. He came roaring right up to the front door on his motorcycle all the way from Albuquerque, and what a welcome sight he was, dead bugs on his face and all. He was as happy to slip into our arms as ever, and we as happy and fulfilled to receive him, not to mention incredibly thankful for his safe arrival.

Since Brian had not departed for his sophomore year at college yet, all of us were once more gathered and sleeping under the same roof. Fellowship was warm, fun-filled, rejuvenating. The boys wrestled on the floor. The phone rang off the hook. The door opened and closed during all hours of the day and night.

I spent several long pauses observing, considering, testing, exploring my own emotions and pondering the actions and reactions of each of us—and all of us as a unit.

Although there were some similarities to the past, it was not like old times. It was more like the beginning of what comes next. Four relatively mature individuals coming face to face and hug to hug. No distinguishing lines between the chiefs and Indians; all equal members of the same tribe; each bearing fragments of what used to be; each learning to respect and accept what has changed.

And should an unacceptable pecking order try to sneak its way back in there, tasteful deterrence is administered. Such was the case after a rather intense phone conversation Brian and I had after he returned to school one time last year. A few days later, the following gentle yet straight-to-the-point announcement arrived in the middle of a letter.

"Don't get me wrong, I still want your advice, but in some areas, wait for me to come to you. Thanks." This was followed by a smiley face.

I am grateful for his diplomacy. It was something I needed to be reminded of. It is another of those treasured pieces of paper I keep in my special notebook. And I was particularly tickled he used one of the tools I taught him to deliver the message: the written word— without the possibility of interruption before the message gets delivered in its entirety. One of the remnants. One of the rewards. See, I told you they're paying attention even when you think they're not!

*   *   *

Of course, emergency phone calls still infiltrate our quiet. Like the one I got around dinner time from Bret one day.

"How long can you keep bratwurst before it rots?" he queried. Ah, the comforts of knowing we are still, in whatever small way, needed. And what a challenge it was trying to explain "that" smell as I passed on my motherly knowledge.

That same simple being-needed pleasure can also be agonizing, especially if the long-distance call concerns a broken heart that cannot be mended by the loving hands or words of a mother or father. I received such a call once.

"I wish you were here to hold me, Mom," the familiar voice quietly said.

I believe none of us ever gets too old to make that wish or too detached to long to fulfill it. Visions of my ninety-year-old grandmother stroking the hair of her bedridden seventy-four-year-old daughter, my aunt, come to mind. No, age has nothing to do with motherly and fatherly love.

But then there are the phone calls that come just to let you know what they've been up to, like the ones I make to and receive from my dad and our children make to and receive from us in return. Sometimes they're just news about the weather, or "I'm bored," or "I'm thinking about you," or "I'm thinking about something else and I'd like to run it by you."

Some of my favorite conversations are the funny, wait-until-you-hear-this-one! stories. But then again, not all of them are funny: Bret recently had his truck stolen. Brian recently ran out of money at school.

But life has its peaks as well:

We all shared the good news that Bret would be home for Christmas.

George finished a long, ongoing fix-it project in the kitchen.

I started up my Bible Study Fellowship classes again.

Brian logged 4.5 hours on a solo flight and everything went well, including communications.

(Another valley, but not a surprise: the flight ran Brian out of money—again.)

We pass the word from one to another, trying to repeat all the details so no one is left out of the family grapevine. George and I pass the phone back and forth, savoring the details and discussing them over dinner.

Of course many things happen in their lives which we will never know about. And that, too, is the way it should be. After all, Dad and I have our secrets!

And speaking of George and me, that *us* of a couple I spoke about earlier, we have discovered that quiet is nice. Very nice. Although the deadening silence in the beginning was hard to handle and a constant reminder of what was not any more, we have now grown to adore it.

We have discovered having the boys living elsewhere gives us more places to visit, aside from Kmart, of course.

We have survived our first summer of having a college student back home after his freshman year. And believe me, that ain't easy! I had been warned about this by many parents more experienced than myself. "Oh, you won't be crying next year when he leaves," they said, trying to console me after we dropped him off that first college year.

"Callous," I thought. "They're so callous. They must not have the kind of relationships with their children that we have with ours."

I have learned that this haughty attitude reaps rewards equal to the "My kids would never . . ." bravado. Yes, we learned to eat crow. We were happy, happy, happy to see him return to school. Although a couple of tears did slip down my cheek at the departure, before they were even dry, I was anxious to once again return to my silent and peaceful house. Except for the interruptions of the barking dog and squawking parakeet. Brian, too, was ready to return to his new-found independent lifestyle. And the 4,783 miles Bret put on his motorcycle this past summer definitely primed him for a sigh of relief when he pulled back into his driveway in Albuquerque.

We've all covered a lot of mental territory the last few years. I'm sure we will continue to grow in our new and ever-changing roles in the future.

*   *   *

It occurs to me as I examine our empty nest that preparing for it, in some ways, begins the minute the child leaves your womb. The tying off of the umbilical cord, severing mother from child, becomes the first step in the process of letting go. Then weaning. Independent steps. Kindergarten. Sock hops. First loves. Driver's license. Graduation. Departure.

The irony is that although you spend your entire life letting go in little, sometimes unaware chunks, it still ends up feeling like a smack of cold water in the face when they actually go.

But like diving into a cold creek, you eventually get used to the water until you no longer feel the cold. In fact, after a long enough time, it becomes the air that is hard to take again. And so it is with the empty nest.

How clever of God to make us so adaptable.

How gracious he is to send friends into our lives who travel our same roads. And now that all our kids are gone, I find the level of our relationships with these friends has somehow deepened. Perhaps it's because we're all getting so mellow with age. Perhaps it's because we have more time to talk to one another—and actually listen to answers—without child-related interruptions.

Of course when we get together, our children are always the first thing discussed. We ask about each one, carefully going through the list and marking their progress—or sometimes lack of.

One couple we know has a twenty-five-year-old college graduate working and living at home. Kids sure have a way of recycling today. Perhaps that's why I'm not panting over Brian's bedroom yet.

Another couple has the husband's mother living with them. She has Alzheimer's disease, and life is not quite what they had pictured. She moved in about the time their baby moved out.

"I was looking forward to not having to be home at a certain time or prepare meals at a certain time—just not to be on a schedule," the wife said. "But I am. So it didn't work out."

Together with our friends, we share the trials and triumphs, the unexpected. We nurture each other and try to fill in some of the gaps. We replay the old days. We look forward to what is ahead.

•

Dear Charlie Brown,
Yes, the Great Pumpkin
Lives! Don't let them
kid you. Keep
spreading the word with
your bountiful joy and
enthusiasm. Others
like ourselves are sure to believe!

•

· *Twelve* ·

Harvest Celebration

The Fruits of Our Labors

The *sound of chirping crickets pierces through the crack under the* overhead door and spreads across the garage floor. It lightly pulsates in our eardrums as we sit cross-legged on the cool cement. The fragrance of burning leaves—those piles of paisley colors—drifts under that same crack and up our noses, subtly announcing the season. It is a fragrance we love, and one that seems to inspire the creative genius in us as we face the blank canvas of pumpkin. Our senses are alive and heightened by the task at hand.

Newspapers cover the floor; pumpkin guts cover a couple of the headlines. A few seeds have already found their way into the colander where they await washing, salting, baking and eating. They are the perfect and annual complement to the fresh-pressed jugs of cider waiting in the fridge.

We are camped far enough apart from one another so that spying is ruled out. Heaven forbid an idea should be copied or a surprise unveiled before its time. Markers, pencils, knives and miscellaneous paraphernalia are scattered around us. We have collected these tools of the pumpkin-carving trade from about the house and yard: perhaps a few corn husks for hair, a bumpy gourd that "warts" can be extracted from, construction paper, yarn . . . implements are tossed back and forth on request.

An occasional snicker skitters through the garage as one of us erupts with enthusiasm for our oh-so-clever idea. Errant indelible black lines and incisions are followed by groans and sighs. Time passes; we are unaware. Our annual fall celebration is in progress.

There we would sit: mother, father and two sons carving their pumpkins. We carried on this behavior far beyond the age, by some standards, fit for pumpkin carving. Although finding a mutually agreeable time became more difficult over the years, enthusiasm never waned for this tradition.

Some things never changed: we always seemed to finish at the same time, thereby accommodating the Great Lighting and Unveiling. And there has always been sincere appreciation for each of our creations. We oohed and aahed at our individual visions-come-to-life. We seemed to take turns generating the most clever of ideas. Each year a new King or Queen Pumpkin Carver grinned while all agreed on the ordination.

As the boys grew older, an occasional newcomer joined us, and they usually wore mascara. It tickled me that Bret and Brian found this celebration grand enough to want to share with their truly beloveds of the time. Of course the celebration encompassed more than pumpkin carving; it included a near-choreographed routine of events. This tradition had begun for me when I was a toddler. I ushered it into my own family with reverence. The boys, in turn, grew up loving the annual trek and celebration as much as I did, and still do. George has a hard time envisioning fall without it now.

It always began with a drive to Johnson's Mound in Elburn. Always taking the same country roads. Speaking of nostalgic remembrances. Entering the winding road into the park. Watching for the carving of the Indian head that mysteriously appeared one year high up one of the trees.

Next stop: the Gould cider farm. We could hardly wait for a fresh taste of the day's pressing. We were given a sample like a fine wine, straight out of the holding barrel. There was never a doubt that a purchase would result. If we were lucky, they would be pressing when we arrived. All those crates of apples hand-dumped onto the mini-conveyor belt powered by a running tractor. Chopped in the chopper. Pressed through layers and layers of burlap. Yield: fresh cider that stifled any question as to why bees hung around the place.

On the way home, pumpkins were purchased and nestled next to the cider in the trunk, just waiting for carving and drinking.

Times have changed somewhat: thank goodness Johnson's Mound and the Gould cider place are still intact, but the country roads aren't quite as country anymore. Bret is never here for Halloween, and pumpkin carving usually takes place around the kitchen table now. We are all older, wiser, more careful, and less able and willing to sit cross-legged on the cold garage floor. Burning paisley fragrance no longer wafts up our noses, what with environmental concerns and all. I imagine that this year the ritual will take place whichever weekend Brian can make it home instead of "the" weekend. If he doesn't make it home during the season, I'm sure George and I will carry on tradition alone. I can't imagine Halloween around our home without cheery or dastardly pumpkin faces staring out from our front porch.

No, I can't imagine that at all, any more than I can imagine dropping the celebration all together, since we are a family that loves to harvest the celebratory fruits. After all, if we don't take time to ceremoniously take in the joyful moments, to in fact *make* some of those moments, what's the point of grinding through the rough times?

Let me just take a second here to define what I mean by a celebration: any conscious act to make something special out of the moment or occasion. This can be as large as an invitations-only party that requires a catering service, or as small as a verbal "Hey! What a moment!" It is a deliberate marking of time.

Children give us natural cause to celebrate. All those "firsts."

*   *   *

"Oh, sweetheart, Jenny smiled at me today!"

"You should have seen Jacob turn over! We've a gymnast in the making, I'm sure of it!"

"Come to Daddy, son. That's right, one wobbly foot in front of the other. You did it!"

"Okay. Let's see it. Yea, Kelly! You went poopoo in the potty!"

Some friends of ours have celebration dinners for good report cards. I like that idea, although I'm glad the Baumbichs didn't have to depend on that for fun. We do, however, make the most out of birthdays. Always have. And what more profound to celebrate than the gift of life?

Like the Gould cider tradition I brought to our family, so I inherited the Birthday Bonanza spirit. I was born into a Birthday Family. The Brown clan cherishes dozens of what we refer to as "puffer fish photographs." It doesn't matter how old or young my mom, dad, brother or I were turning, there we are, frozen in time. Cheeks flared out like a bellows, eyebrows scrunched together, face about one foot away from torching our hair on the candles, a dorky pointed hat perched on our head, wishes dangling in the air, the official pink-and-blue crepe-paper Happy Birthday streamer scotch-taped to the wall in the background. Birthday Heaven indeed!

It wouldn't have made a lick of sense if I didn't usher all this excitement into my own family, including spanking the birthday person one gentle swat for each year, plus "one to grow on." And so, of course, I did. What wonderful memories the array of birthday parties alone has left us.

One of the first that stands out was when Brian turned one year old. We have nearly worn out that short-playing, eight-millimeter piece of film over the years. And each time we laugh ourselves silly. Each year that memory becomes more precious.

*   *   *

There sits Brian in his yellow, flowered, vinyl-covered high chair. He is wearing only a tee shirt and disposable diaper, a big grin and of course a dorky birthday hat with an elastic strap encircling his beaming little face. George's large hand enters the right side of the frame and swiftly sets the pint-sized chocolate cake down in front of him. I used an old chicken-pot-pie tin as a cake pan for this masterpiece. One candle glows atop the extra thick chocolate frosting.

Brian studies it for a moment, then looks up into the camera because everyone over in that direction is instructing and coaxing him to blow it out—as well as charading. We constituted a puffer fish

179

ensemble, you might say. Too bad the camera was facing in the wrong direction. Anyway, pretty soon he blows it out and we all clap and so does he. Next we start urging him to eat some cake.

At first he is a little cautious. One finger punctures the top of the cake like a meat thermometer. Then he gives the sticky goo a lick. Yummm. Like an industrial crane set to motion, his fat little hand engages, scoops out a giant helping, crams it into his mouth. This is where the picture starts bouncing up and down a tad. I have yet to learn how to keep laughter contained to my face.

As he chews and reshuffles the escaping bits, we see the candle start to disappear into his mouth like a sucked-up spaghetti noodle. This is where there is a gap in the film.

The closing shot captures the last morsel off the plate being crammed into an already full mouth. He is chocolate from ear to ear. His little toes are turned up and looking happy like the rest of him.

* * *

The next birthday occasion that comes to mind is Bret's second-grade party—to which silly us invited his entire class. What I remember best about this party is that the basement housed a state of chaos for two full hours. Bret was so overwhelmed with it, it was hard to tell if he was even having a good time. We learned something here: Birthday Happiness is not created by sheer numbers.

* * *

Next comes the magic-show birthday. It was the year Brian wanted to decorate his own cake and he used every cake decorating doo-dah in our house, including ten one-inch American flags. Let's just say that due to cake crowding, we experienced flag burning before it became newsworthy. Ours, of course, was accidental. This was not the magic part, however.

The magic part came right after the pizza party. Since Brian's birthday is December 30, Christmas gifts are still a novelty, and Bret had received a wonderful magic-show kit under the tree. Thus, the need for an audience—aside from his family who were, five days into around-the-clock entertainment, sick and tired of magic. And so, six six-year-olds gathered around the young magician who wore his hair in bangs. They sat spellbound—for about three minutes. Then they wanted cake. So much for the "magic" birthday.

*   *   *

I could go on and on telling birthday stories, but they are *obvious* reasons for celebrating. More important to the celebration tally of things are the less formal occasions, because they can gallop in at any unsuspecting moment. I'm talking about little out-of-the-ordinary bursts of things to be joyful about. And like most things, perhaps experiencing them has to do with attitude.

". . . the cheerful heart has a continual feast," reads Proverbs 15:15. I believe a cheerful heart is a hot wire to joy. And, "A cheerful heart is good medicine" (Prov 17:22).

In order to teach your children to have a joyful heart, you must first learn how yourself. Learn to take notice of the little things worthy of celebration.

"Even though I've made meat loaf a thousand times, this time it just seems perfect!"

"My boss bragged about my productivity at a meeting today!"

"This is a brand new permanent and I'm not devastated!"

"Look, everybody! The row of beans I planted last week is sprouting!"

181

"Can you believe it? I won the pie-eating contest at the Fourth of July fest! My name is going to be in the newspapers!"

Okay. So this last announcement didn't evoke quite the response I thought it would. But then it's not *my* fault they found my latest achievement embarrassing.

Usually, however, everyone perked up when the celebratory tone echoed throughout our household. It didn't matter who used it; it brought bursts of energy into otherwise routine days. A mini-celebration reminded everyone that life is more than cooking, cleaning your room, mowing, homework, raising kids. It sometimes even brought new meaning to those "ordinary" things.

Long ago, the writer of Ecclesiastes said, "I know that there is nothing better for men [and women, and children] than to be happy and do good while they live. That everyone may eat and drink, and find satisfaction in all his toil—this is the gift of God" (3:12-13). Life *is* worth celebrating, isn't it.

Take notice of the small miracles: A Popsicle that *didn't* drip all over the newly scrubbed floor. A lawn mower's sharpened blade which sheared the perfect path. A cookie recipe that honestly made as many cookies as the recipe said it would. (Okay, I'm still waiting for this one. But I believe it's possible!)

A baby who smiled on cue. Legos that snapped together into the perfect automobile. A sparkly rock that was delivered in the load of gravel. A knock-knock joke that was actually funny. A part in the school play. The smell of a bouquet of flowers—even though they were picked by tiny hands from a neighbor's yard. One brother patting the other on the back in a sign of consolation and love. A neatly folded basket of laundry. A hug when you need one.

Many of our friends have found one-on-one occasions are always cause for celebration. The night Daddy takes just one of his daughters for ice cream. The day Mom treats her middle son to miniature golf. The fishing trip a first-born spends alone with Dad or Mom. A special time when a child doesn't have to share the limelight or the parent. Dates are made and put on the calendar. Minds are cleared. Sharing is heard. These "dates" are remembered; I've heard that validated by parents and grown children alike.

*   *   *

All celebrations aren't cheery. The day Bret moved to Albuquerque isn't high up there on my list of singing and clapping times. You already know I am a weeper; we're talking rivers-full here.

But there he sat behind the wheel of his giant old green car that was packed to the gills and riding low. He was smiling, but anticipation and nervousness danced on his face. It was a look I had grown familiar with and quite attached to. It captured his face any time he brought us news that he knew would be met with mixed emotions.

I swear, I could see his heart beating in his eyes. His precious giving heart. The one I'm sure I errantly missed sometimes in the heat of the moment. But this time it couldn't be missed. And it nearly tugged mine out of my chest.

I couldn't help but crack a warm-hearted smile at his final get-ready. He hopped out of his car, rummaged through something in the trunk and produced his rebel flag that had adorned his bedroom wall for so many years. He ceremoniously unfolded it and draped it over his "stuff" in the back seat, carefully tucking it in. "The One And Only." Flying his rebel flag across the country.

"God's speed," I prayed as he backed out of the drive following about eleventy-dozen hugs.

And yet it was a celebration. The marking of time when a man followed his heart's desire.

*   *   *

So many markings of time. And then they're gone.

I find that I have now entered my grandmother wonderment phase. No, as of this writing there are none on the way—thank goodness, because neither son is married. Yet I find myself anxious for this passage of our lives.

You see, I collect crystal prisms that hang in my windows. Most are pieces of old chandeliers that I have picked up at antique shops or garage sales. Some are that Austrian full-leaded crystal that hangs in shopping malls, its sparkly beauty capturing my attention, then my pocketbook.

Please don't confuse this hobby of mine with the "new age" use of crystals. The attention that has been drawn to quartz crystals and their "powers" is totally removed from the simple pleasure I gain by seeing God-given light refracted through a crystal, then cast into beautiful rainbows around my house.

And I do mean "around my house." They hang from fish line in windows on nearly all sides, ever waiting to capture the sun as it moves past. I have seen a drab flower arrangement burst into colorful splendor. I have seen green, red and blue stripes perch on Butch's nose. I have watched my friend's baby stop in mid-crawl to try to scoop one of the colorful curiosities up off the floor, only to find it settling on the back of his hand.

One of my favorites took place the day I was baking lasagna. When I opened the oven door, a burst of color branded my bubbling dinner, thereby opening an entire chain of fanciful thinking:

*   *   *

I hope some day my grandchildren will be excited about coming to Granny's house so they can sit in her magic kitchen and eat cookies baked with rainbows inside them.

We will sit together—a sweet-smelling child on each of my knees—and simply be in wonder at slices of rainbows that gently peel off the sun's rays and land on ordinary objects, making them become extraordinary jewels kissed with the hope that All Can Become More Than It Appears. And I will use that beautiful image to tell them about my Lord, the Creator of Rainbows, and the power he has to make all this happen—and more.

Visions of wonderment dance in my head: baby at my beautiful daughter-in-law's breast. Tiny fingers wrapped around larger, caring ones. My sons looking over their beloved wives' shoulders. Finger paintings sent to Grandma and Grandpa to hang on their refrigerator door. Best batting average on the baseball team. Captain of a major airline . . .

And then they'll bring them over to visit.

And leave them screaming at the door. And they will dirty their pants. And tell me they love me. And track mud on the new carpet Grandpa and I just got. And curl in our laps while we read stories.

And we will study the similarities in the faces of our children and grandchildren, and maybe spy a slight resemblance to ourselves.

And they will have very good days and very bad days. And their parents will take them home and we will sigh with blessed relief and joy. And we will look ever so forward to their return.

And wonderment will take on a whole new meaning. And entire new volumes of memories in our old-age portfolios will be spread before our aged friends at bingo games.

And I wouldn't miss these children for the world, any more than I missed my own.